A MODEL OF INTERPERSONAL SPEECH COMMUNICATION

Paul E. Ried

UNIVERSITY
PRESS OF
AMERICA

Copyright © 1979 by
University Press of America, Inc.™
P.O. Box 19101, Washington, D.C. 20036

All rights reserved

Printed in the United States of America

ISBN (Perfect): 0-8191-0755-7

Library of Congress Number: 79-64197

To Marjorie

PREFACE

This monograph is designed to explicate a model of interpersonal speech communication for introductory courses in speech communication. The model is theoretical, but based on the author's observations and experiences over thirty years of teaching. The uses to which such a model can be put are: 1) helping the practitioner of the art to become more communicative, 2) aiding the teacher to better prepare students to communicate, and 3) guiding researchers in their attempts to increase understanding of what happens when communication does take place. It is felt that these advantages can be realized when the model presented here is understood. What is unusual about this model is its philosophical base, an understanding of people which, despite its importance in the history of Western thought, has been overlooked in communication theory. The model also includes a categorization of designs never before essayed. These designs or approaches to people are geared to the goal of equality not dominance-submission in human relationships.

It is hoped that those persons who study this model will be moved to improve upon it, and that such improvements will be conveyed amicably to the author. Appreciation is here given to the editors of Communication Education for permission to use portions of the article "A Spectrum of Persuasive Design," published in the March, 1964 issue of the journal when it was entitled The Speech Teacher.

Paul E. Ried
Syracuse University
January, 1979

TABLE OF CONTENTS

	Page
INTRODUCTION.	1

PART I: PEOPLE IN SPEECH COMMUNICATION

Classical Perspective.	3
Contemporary Perspective	5
Processes in Communication	8
The Creative Processes.	11
Imagination.	11
Designation.	12
Extemporization.	13
The Critical Processes.	16
Interpretation	16
Disposition.	18
Evaluation	19
Adaptive Action: A Synthesis. . .	19

PART II: PATTERNS IN SPEECH COMMUNICATION

Historical Perspective	23
Designs.	25
Directive Designs	27
Dictation.	27
Advocation	28
Dualation.	30
Non-directive Designs	32
Interrogation.	32
Description.	33
Causation.	34
Indirective Designs	36
Parastation.	38
Problemation	43
Coalation.	49

Page

PART III: PRACTICE IN SPEECH COMMUNICATION

    Dimensions of Strength/Weakness... 58
        Individual Dimensions 58
            Knowledge........... 58
            Interest 59
            Emotional Stability...... 60
            Belief 60
            Activity 61
        Social Influences 61
        Cultural Background 63
    Dimension of Cooperation/
            Competition...... 66
    Techniques for Measuring
            Dimensions 67
    Relating Patterns to People..... 69
    Relating Delivery to Design..... 76

CONCLUSION................. 79

FIGURES

    Positions in Speech Communication 9
    A Spectrum of Communication Design..... 37
    Designs Related to Positions........ 70

These figures were developed with the help of Carolyn Coit.

INTRODUCTION

Models of communication or rhetorics have had a long history in the Western world, dating from the dialogues of Plato to contemporary communication theories in twentieth-century American texts. The best of the models appearing over this twenty-five hundred year span have been developed by theorists who have recognized with Plato that a unified theory of communication should provide the following: 1) a general understanding of human beings and how they function in society, 2) a broadly-based understanding of approaches available to the person who wishes to communicate, and 3) clear guidelines concerning which approach is best with whom under what circumstances.

Each age in history has produced its own view of human behavior, and perceptive rhetoricians of each period have adapted their theories to practices consonant with these views. Accordingly, major advances made in Western rhetoric appear to coincide with quantum leaps made in understanding human behavior. They are associated specifically with Greek and Roman theory of the classical period, the British-Scottish rhetorical renascence culminating in the Eighteenth Century, and, finally, American communication theory of the Twentieth Century. Each of these periods produced an unusual expansion of the boundaries of communication theory. The theorists of the classical period saw the communicator persuading others to accept his own ideas. Eighteenth-century Scottish theorists viewed the communicator as achieving purposes with others who, in turn, were able to respond in terms of their own needs and goals. In the United States of the past three decades, listeners have been seen more and more as the first or initiating force in communication. In a sense, the processes of speaking and listening have been viewed as interchangeable to the point where the communicator and communicatee are thought of as indistinguishable.

Rather than starting with the speaker's purposes and treating methods by which those purposes are achieved with others, modern communication theorists have tended to start with the relative positions of persons in communication with the thought that these positions should be brought into balance through ideas of mutual benefit. Communication has come to be thought of as the <u>great equalizer</u> in human relationships, and it is so defined here. Communication is the process by which strength is shared, where persons accept ideas of benefit to enhance their own lives and to aid their society and their world. Speech communication is simply that form of communication which employs speech.

In practical terms, the model offered here is designed to increase the probabilities of a person's using an approach appropriate to giving up or seeking the strength necessary to establish a balance of power in interpersonal relationships. A synthesis or a combination of purposes is sought to achieve mutual benefits. Part I of this model explains people and processes in communication. Part II covers the patterns or tactics available to the communicator, and Part III treats the practice of relating people and patterns in real-life persuasion. Qualifications and a summary are included in a brief concluding section.

PART I

PEOPLE IN SPEECH COMMUNICATION

Classical Perspective

Since the beginning, communication theorists have been preoccupied with the nature of the human soul. This concern was first established in Western theory by Plato's belief that an understanding of the psyche, the self, or the being of man constitutes the speaker's first requisite, and, without this understanding, a speaker remains ignorant of the means of "enchanting the soul," the end, Plato felt, of persuasive discourse. Speech theorists have consistently urged that students of communication study themselves and others to the end Plato suggests.

In the _Phaedrus_, Plato sketched his own view of the human psyche by describing a person as a composite of critically ordered reason, creatively turbulent emotion, and an adjusting, active will. By poetic analogy, he compared the soul to two horses and a chariot and a charioteer; the charioteer's role consists of managing the divergent characters of these two horses as they pull the chariot toward the realm of truth. One horse is finely made, a thoroughbred who responds quickly to the touch of the rein. The other is an ungainly, half-wild beast whose only desire is the irresponsible pursuit of pleasure. The latter's unruly tendencies, in contrast to his partner's patience, results in obvious confusion for the charioteer. The thoroughbred might be compared to reason, intellect, humanity's socializing and most distinctive characteristic. The other horse might be compared to the emotive side of the human being, desires, feelings, and residual animal instincts. The charioteer is representative of the active, willing, moral agent which is immediately and directly responsible for the individual's social behavior.

These components of human nature, reason, emotion, and activity, have been underscored by many important philosophers in the Western tradition. Note Aristotle's classic divisions of logos, pathos, and ethos; the faculty psychologist's predilection for mind, passion, and will; the late-nineteenth and early-twentieth century popularization of the terms, thinking, feeling, and acting; and the contemporary psychological classifications of the cognitive, affective, and enactive domains in human growth and development.

The similarities between this picture of the human soul and modern psychoanalytic theory are indeed apparent. Sigmund Freud, we know, was a student of the classics, and it is unlikely he failed to note Plato's view of the soul in the Phaedrus. Whether a direct tie between the two exists or not, Freud's portrait of the human psyche parallels point by point Plato's analogy of the charioteer. The unconscious id and superego comprise a person's desires and social conscience, a span as paradoxical as Plato's team of horses; the conscious ego compares to the mediations of the charioteer whom Plato placed prominently in view above and between the other two.

More recently, Eric Berne theorizes on the basis of hundreds of case studies that three conscious states, comparable to the id, superego, and ego, exist, and that they may be appropriately termed the child, the parent, and the adult. Each has a role relative to the others, and each participates in the individual's ultimate behavior. Put in another way, what people want to do and what they think they should do are distinct tendencies, sometimes consonant, sometimes contradictory, but what they do represents patently the operations of a third agency in latent concert with these tendencies, all communicating under the individual's own skin. To illustrate, the internal child, on impulse, may desire a given object, and the internal parent may believe it to be undesirable. If the object, for example, is an ice-cream sundae, the parent could argue that it is weight-producing and harmful to the teeth. The adult is positioned between the child and the parent and mediates, perhaps synthesizing different objectives. As the ensuing discussion ends, other persons in a drugstore might observe this person avoiding the ice-cream counter and buying a roll of life-savers, satisfying the child and providing answers to the parent's objections.

Contemporary Perspective

In the modern world the child is thought of as relatively weak or subordinate; the parent is thought of as strong or superior; and the adult might be thought of as an equal to the others combined, but of, by, and for both of them. These power relationships suggest distinguishing characteristics which might be grouped as follows:

superior	equal	subordinate
conservative	moderate	liberal
protective	promotive	provocative
judicial	executive	legislative
reflective	articulative	impulsive
objective	interjective	subjective
scientific	rhetorical	poetic
other-directed	idea-directed	self-directed
critical	adaptive-active	creative

These three lists of characteristics might be subsumed respectively under three processes in persuasion: critical reflection, adaptive action, and creative impulse. An individual personality may reveal emphasis of any one of these processes and may be characterized in communication with others as critical, adaptive-active, or creative. Over a period of time, a person may assume many interpersonal postures ranging from critic to creator. But

an average or typical tendency can be determined,
and a person can be typed accordingly on three
distinctly different levels: 1) the intrapersonal
level, or communication under the individual's own
skin, 2) the interpersonal level, or communication
between communicators and communicatees, person-to-
person, on the social level, and 3) the extrapersonal level, or communication between groups, teams,
nations, cultures, and hemispheres. This last
level usually requires mechanization of some sort,
a television set, radio, movie camera, etc., etc.

In the normal family situation where relationships are interpersonal but often private in nature,
tendencies toward the creative, the critical, and
the adaptive-active are especially pronounced. When
the parent and child communicate, the relationship
between them is clearly a relationship between the
strong and the weak, particularly if the parent is
thirty-three years old and the son or daughter is
two. The relationship between the modern husband
and wife, on the other hand, is often characterized
by equality. The equilibrium explicit in the balance
of power in this relationship changes as different
subjects are discussed, but the average of communication transactions should, according to the ideal
picture, remain balanced or equal. If this balance
is skewed in one direction or the other consistently,
a relationship based on dominance-subordination
develops.

When the individual moves from the family
situation into the more public social life of the
community, relationships become less clear-cut and
more difficult to assess. The strength-weakness
dimension is complicated by another important dimension which might be viewed as cooperation-competition
or, in the extreme, friendliness-hostility. The belief that social relationships differ from familial
relationships in this way results from the assump-
tion that a person in a normal family tends to
cooperate, but it may be that some persons are better
prepared for the social scene by a family life which

is laced with competition. In any case, the strength-weakness relationships outside the home are initially more subtle than those associated with homelife. When two independent adults in a democratic society or when two sixteen year olds from the same neighborhood meet, a basic equality is presumed. These presumptions are subject to quick change at any time, and the changes may result from totally different causes. The sixteen year olds may adjust positions due to physical size and strength. The adults may assume positions based on social status, income, or some other commonly recognized value.

In the process of building human relationships, positions emerge which do not represent equality. Those persons who become the "haves" of society tend to perpetuate their socially recognized strengths presumably to increase their independence of action. Those who become "have-nots" seem to habituate behaviors which make them dependent upon others. This condition tends to be reinforced by the isolation of one group from the other. The strong are less apt to be observed listening. To reverse a well-worn phrase, they are heard but not seen. The weak tend to be seen but not heard. This kind of silence-inducing isolation results in greater imbalance of positions. A re-ordering of communications is necessary if movement toward isolation is to be reversed. The weak must speak as well as listen, and the strong must listen as well as speak. The weak must create if the strong are to respond openly. Viewed from this perspective, communication can indeed be the great equalizer. It can aid in the establishment and maintenance of an ideal balance of power in human relations.

Put in another more practical and political context, the conservative, critical "haves" protect the status quo and protect other conservatives. These persons are associated with strength and are traditionally given the presumption in human transactions. The "have-nots" are liberal, creative types who, having little investment in the status quo, seek change. They operate initially from a position of weakness which becomes stronger when they present a <u>prima</u> <u>facie</u> case. This case, by the way, can be communicated in many ways. It may come in the form of a crowd shouting loudly for reform, visual and vocal symbolization of a need for change. Or it may be verbalized quietly and rationally in forums designed specifically to legislate social change. Breaking into society, the market place, the centers of power demands of the have-nots the development of their creative powers. In other words, then, ideas must be made sufficiently attractive to a majority of people in order to effect change in society.

Processes in Speech Communication

On the intrapersonal level, the child is most closely concerned with provocation through creative processes, and the parent is associated with protection on the basis of critical processes. An individual acts and reacts on the interpersonal level through the agency of the adult, but only after the adult has communicated on the intrapersonal level with the child and the parent. By the same token, interpersonal communication precedes communication on the extrapersonal level. On any level, however, communication processes are best understood as a sequential series of episodes in the human being's development of a quality idea.

Before an idea moves a single individual to adaptive action on the interpersonal level, then, it has already passed through a series of creative impulses and critical reflections, through two parallel but, in another sense, antagonistic sets of processes: creative, childlike, synthesizing processes and critical, parental, analyzing processes. The creative processes are discussed here as imagination, designation, and extemporization. Corresponding critical processes are interpretation, disposition, and evaluation. These two sets of pro-

✷ THE COMMUNICATOR

POSITIONS IN COMMUNICATION

cesses, operating in concert or in competition within
the individual, lead to adaptive action on the interpersonal level. If emphasis in communication is on
adaptation, the person listens; if the emphasis is on
action, the person speaks.

At the outset of communication on the interpersonal level, especially in written communication,
the communicator assumes the creative role, and the
communicatee assumes the critical role. From that
point in time in speech communication, however, the
roles become so interlaced, spliced, and reshuffled
that both the original speaker and the original listener would have to detach themselves from the communicative act to know which role each is taking.
The complicated nature of communication becomes
clear when it is noted that both the listener and
speaker on the interpersonal level simultaneously
engage in both the creative and critical processes
relative to each other. The speaker's extemporization of a designed image immediately arouses critical
interpretation in the listener. As the speaker extemporizes an idea actively, however, the speaker
also interprets, disposes, and evaluates the listener's behavior, thereby adapting critically. That
is, as the speaker cuts an image out of time and
space with verbal, vocal, visual, and visceral symbols, the listener's behavior is evaluated with an
eye to whether or not these symbols are portraying
the image as clearly as possible for the listener.
While the speaker acts as a speaker, he or she reacts to the listener.

In the same split second that the listener
receives, he or she begins to speak to the speaker.
While interpreting, disposing, and evaluating the
speaker's idea, the listener is already involved in
the creative processes, and, if the listener reaches
extemporization and action, the social roles are
recycled: the speaker becomes the listener, and the
listener becomes the speaker. Human beings have the
capacity to communicate as speaker and listener

simultaneously on three different levels of communication, already mentioned as intrapersonal, interpersonal, and extrapersonal.

An observer of communication on the interpersonal level must set these complications aside, initially at least. The creative processes are speaker related, and the critical processes are listener related. Social traditions in the communication arts make this necessary. As any society becomes large and its structure complicated, communication takes on a ceremonial aspect which standardizes social roles. It is impossible for a political candidate, a professor, or a minister, as examples, to sit and converse informally with each potential listener individually.

It should be noted that as an audience becomes larger, the format of communication becomes more highly structured. A panel discussion, a formal debate, a legitimate play, each progressively limits to a greater degree the speaker's creative processes and the listener's critical processes. The theorem is suggested that the more people and geographic space involved in the communicative situation, the less time there is available for the actual communication to take place. The communicator and the communicatee must spend more time and energy in preparation. Conversely, fewer people occupying less space are permitted more time for active communication, and they require less time for preparation. One-to-one interviewing, according to this hypothesis, allows greatest flexibility in interpersonal communication. The two persons communicating may change roles from speaker to listener with greatest frequency and freedom.

The Creative Processes

1. *Imagination* Whether by conception or perception, human beings tend to fix attention upon images. These may be simple representations of

objects in the environment or highly impressionistic abstractions generated from mental or internal associations. [In the second instance, mental images may appear disjointed in the mind's eye, perhaps superimposed, sometimes multidimensional, moving, all with little rhyme or reason. Walking leaves, busy drones, talking hats, and golden mountains might all be seen in a mental fantasy with the plot complexity of a Shakespearean comedy.

For this reason, imagination has been aligned with childlike fancy, dreams, and half-conscious states where dim pictures of ideas take shape. Often, images in their earliest stages are vague, faint forms which defy description. They are not always born whole. Their life-spans vary from a momentary flicker to long-term brilliance; their movements are sometimes slow and ponderous, at other times elusive and swift. However, the miscellaneous pieces of an image, strewn about on the unconscious levels, somehow merge long enough for designation and extemporization to occur.

Putting these images to work involves the need to stay with them. Mental pictures demand time and warmth for incubation. They must be juggled, reversed, rearranged, turned inside out, chopped up, and magnified. Communicators must permit themselves to be caught up in them. In a childlike (not childish) fashion, they must engage themselves subjectively with the pictures visualized, however fantastic they might be.

2. <u>Designation</u> The process of imagination gradually merges with the second creative process, designation. As the pieces of an image come together, a design or pattern evolves relative to the communicator's self-image, his image of the communicatee, time, place, and the means of symbolization available.

Line, mass, form, and color comprise the tools

of design in visual communication, and the communicator uses them when employing charts, pictures, and models to map an idea. In verbal communication, however, pictorial dimensions of images are transformed into verbal design by the tactical placement of central idea, main ideas, sub-main ideas, etc., within a given communique. In other words, an image may have many dimensions, and making each dimension clear verbally while relating it to other dimensions requires a patterning or clustering of ideas within a given speech. An examination of specific types of design available to the speaker is taken up in Part II of this work. Suffice it here to say that these designs range from the question mark to the exclamation point, from non-directive through indirective to directive designs. If the image or picture the communicator is translating into verbal design is, relative to listener, time, place, and means, a well-drawn, firmly set idea, verbal design tends toward direction. A superior to subordinate relationship is implied in this design. If the picture the communicator sees is newly formed, dim, or vague, verbal design tends generally toward non-direction. A subordinate to superior relationship is anticipated by the speaker. If both persons communicating are in the same stages relative to the formation of the idea and see each other as equals, indirect verbal designs usually result based on an equal to equal relationship. When two equals cease to cooperate and begin to argue an idea, both see themselves as superior to the other person and each assumes a directive stance toward the other. They might still be viewed by an observer as equals.

    3. *Extemporization* The creative process of extemporization edges into the growth of an idea when the communicator attempts to convert a designed image into verbal, visual, vocal, and visceral symbols for others. The speaker cuts out of time or transfixes the designed image so that others may see it as he or she sees it, knowing that the symbols available always result to some degree in oversimplification. At

some point the communicator is forced by the very symbols used, however skillfully, to select portions of ideas for communication. It is hoped an equally imaginative communicatee will fill in the gaps left by symbols both recognize as less than completely adequate.

Yet, if an imaginative individual cannot express ideas with practical effect, they are worthless to others. An idea short of adaptive action is not a complete idea, in which case the act of communication remains in limbo, unfinished. The symbolic implications of a designed image may never open up sufficiently to permit extemporization to others. The communicator's own critical processes may cut off creative efforts; listening to the parent, the speaker may refuse to move from designation to extemporization.

To offset this blockage and the partial nature of various kinds of symbols, the communicator must recognize the strengths and weaknesses of each type so that proper combinations can be employed.

Cutting across many images, for example, moves the speaker away from visual extemporization and into the province of the verbal. When only visual symbols are used to extemporize an image, the process compares to a slow, detailed floodlight search of one specific image. The territory of the image can be covered inch by inch with relative completeness. Verbal extemporization compares to a swiftly moving spotlight which covers a great deal more ground but in less detail. Words also permit the inclusion of the concept of time.

It is significant that the earliest written languages on record are based on pictures. Egyptian hieroglyphics and Chinese pictograms and ideograms seem to contain a weakness inherent in pictorial language. Learning and utilizing this form of written language is uneconomical, cumbersome, and space wasting. The phonetically based alphabet which superseded earlier forms of written language saves time and space, and this, in part, accounts for a standard of living in the Western world vastly superior to that of the Orient. Apparently, the achievements of a given culture, the security of its people, and the relative ease with which life is sustained in that culture bear a direct relationship to the speed and sureness of learning the culture's communicative symbols. A culture cannot extend beyond the limits of its lines of communication and, so, the outer fringes of a culture locate for a communicator the point where most interpersonal communication terminates.

When the communicator comes into the presence of an audience, he or she also brings muscle tensions, sweat, itches, and all of those visceral conditions which communicate. When speakers scratch, droop, twitch, straighten, and twist, they give cues about the strength of their attachment to the ideas they are attempting to present. Any symbol which conveys involvement or preoccupation communicates to others; a wet shirt, for example, may carry more meaning than any picture or word. Under most conditions, aromas and various forms of physical contact transmit emotional meanings lacking in other forms of symbolization. The visceral forms of symbolization, then, portend their own special strengths for the speaker.

The human voice is also especially capable of transmitting unique emotive dimensions of images. Acceptance and rejection register easily in vocal patterns brought about by variety in rate, pitch, quality, and volume. Subtle configurations of feeling, personal likes and dislikes cannot be better symbolized than vocally even when the communicator is physically distant or out of sight of the audience as in the cases of the radio and the telephone.

The recent history of live Broadway productions reveals that ideas are most effectively extemporized when visual, verbal, vocal and visceral means are unified simultaneously. Note the pre-eminence of the modern musical comedy. Television has superseded radio for the same reason. The point is this. While each type of symbolization has its special strength, the more types which can honestly be brought to bear on an idea, the more effective the transmission of the idea will be with the greatest number of people.

The Critical Processes

1. *Interpretation* Interpretation is the first critical process by which an idea is analyzed to determine its validity and its significance. As a critical listener, the individual's interpretative analysis proceeds in terms of the symbols chosen by the speaker to depict the designed image. Consequently, the listener must ask what the symbols denote and connote before disposition (classification) and evaluation can occur. A communicator's extemporization may be interpreted, then, on a number of levels. The speaker may, for example, recount on an interpersonal level what has significance solely on the intrapersonal level. The husband who says to his wife, "You don't care for me any more," may actually mean, "I am angry." He may be describing an internal state, not a socially significant fact or feeling. Then, too, an idea which a communicator extemporizes may have significance only on the broadest, extrapersonal level. Again, the communicatee may interpret it as having no significance to the immediate situation. Speculation is possible if the limitations are recognized; most people communicating about "world peace," for example, have a miniscule influence on the level necessary to aid in directly achieving it.

An extemporized image may have immediate denotative relevance to the social situation at hand.

If it is so interpreted by the communicatee, the image may serve as the basis for the mutual pursuit of an idea. The listener may disagree on the basis of interpretation and communicate a different point of view. Clear interpretation, in other words, may lead to the understanding that two people truly differ, and they may terminate the discussion by mutual agreement to disagree.

In these ways, relative positions are partially established on the interpersonal level. Under agreeable circumstances, the communicatee tends to react as critic when the communicator describes internal states, as co-creator on the extrapersonal level, and as equal when aiding in the promotion of ideas on the immediate interpersonal level.

The communicatee also interprets a communique in relation to the time and place of its utterance. It is presumed that the communicator's efforts are bound by specific time limits. This restriction, measured clock time, imposes upon both the speaker and listener the need to select the most salient features of the idea they follow in communication. This selectivity allows the individual to experience a relatively complete picture through a telescoped sequence of points in time and space. When a real estate salesman shows prospective clients through a house, he or she has the ear of the customer for a limited amount of time. Presumably, the most typical features of the house are selected in the coverage, since a fully detailed verbal description of the house might take days of clock time. The customer interprets the salesman's guided tour with these time and space factors in mind and asks: Has the communicator taken enough time? Too much time? Are points of emphasis well spaced? Are points appropriately selected? Have the specific points of emphasis given a view of the whole house in detail?

Another question the customer asks is: How

honest is the salesman's representation of the
house? Put in another way, has mutual benefit
been foremost in his mind? If the salesman has
perverted communication by seeking benefits, for
example, an unrealistically big price, without regard for the customer's well-being, he has engaged
in propaganda, not persuasion. If, on the other
hand, the customer benefits without reciprocal benefits for the salesman, if the salesman "gives" the
house away, then he has prostituted himself, not
persuaded. Classifications based upon interpretation become important to the listener as he moves
to the next critical process, disposition.

    2. <u>Disposition</u> During the process of inter-
pretation, two basic kinds of disposition begin to
evolve. The internal parts of the communique are
first disposed or classified; the communicatee
analyzes the communicator's message to establish
central idea, main ideas, sub-main ideas, and supporting materials. It should be noted the difference, which will be further distinguished in Part II,
between designation and disposition is the difference between patterning the blueprint of a speech
and the categorization of types of materials imple-
menting that pattern. Designation is a creative
synthesizing of the speech's parts; disposition is
the critical analysis of the speech to arrive at the
classification of those parts.

    The communique is also classified with external
reference. When heard, read, observed, and interpreted, a communicated idea is classified as to type,
genus, and species. A realistic play, to illustrate,
is classified on the first level with other speci-
mens of dramatic realism as distinct from expres-
sionistic plays. This process is crucial to evaluation, the last critical process. Evaluation depends
upon precision of classification. Apples and oranges
are both fruit and can be compared, but the grouping
here is relatively crude. It is simpler to compare
and evaluate the relative merits of two apples. It

is still simpler to evaluate two MacIntoshes. If
classification is impossible, comparison is impossible.
One of a kind can never be evaluated; the first
human being on earth was an "island unto himself," a
Robinson Crusoe without a Friday, a creator without
critics, and evaluation would necessarily await other
human beings with whom he could be compared.

3. <u>Evaluation</u> Evaluation aims at judging the
worth of an idea as it is communicated; an extemporized,
designed image is set beside other comparable
ideas and assigned a relative value. The critic asks:
How much value or benefit does the idea provide? Then
the questions arise: What is the standard of value
employed? What criteria determine whether or not the
standard is met?

A critical acceptance of an idea rests ultimately
on a belief that it has viability, i.e., life
sustaining qualities. This value underlies all
other values held by human beings, regardless of
cultural inheritance and social pressures. It is
true, of course, that people see life in different
ways, but all see life itself as a value basic to
everything else. Criteria for judgment in communication
are subordinated to this standard; an idea to
be of greatest value must provide the most people
with the most benefit. When a communicatee accepts
an idea, acts upon it, and benefits as a result,
i.e., lives more fully, he accords the idea critical
approval. The more benefit which accrues to the
individual, the greater the approval. The good drama,
the good speech, the good TV broadcast all have this
one common denominator: the idea communicated provides
life producing benefits to both the communicator
and the communicatee when they adapt it to their
environment or act upon it to alter that environment.

Adaptive Action: A Synthesis

The development of an idea through the creative
processes of imagination, designation, and

extemporization does not preclude skill in the critical processes of interpretation, disposition, and evaluation. A dual proficiency is necessary because both kinds of processes are essential to quality ideas. On the intrapersonal level, the dreams and impulses in the individual are given perspective and balanced by the critic's perception of reality. Youthful fancy does not take reality into full consideration; therefore images are built on the ideal the desirable, or what should be regardless of what is. Experience registers fact; the critic reflects what is, the real, the practicable. Adult verbal behavior and/or adaptive action represents a compromise or a synthesis between the ideal and the real, what should be and what is, what is desirable and what is practicable. William James developed this idea when he defined a person's sense of success as the ratio between what he feels he is and what he thinks he should be. The inference is that adult patterns of behavior exist somewhere between best intentions and meanest desires.

On the interpersonal level, the listener interprets, disposes, and evaluates the idea as it is represented in symbolic form, a result of imagination, designation, and extemporization. Again, a balance of creative processes attributed initially to the communicator and the critical processes attributed to the communicatee has been described as the source of quality ideas which move speaker and listener alike to actions/adaptations on the social level. At this point, the story of an idea's development reaches its last chapter on the interpersonal level; the idea may, however, extend its influence beyond interpersonal communication. It may have value in the dialogue which occurs between representative leaders of groups and nations. A communicator may speak through others.

This is exemplified in public debate. Initially, affirmative debaters, advocating change in the status quo, function as child-creators; negative debaters take a parental-critical role. But in refutation and rebuttal, these functions become the properties of both sides. While the judge or audience initially forms the third point in the triangle, adult-actors, the audience is finally asked to feel, think, and act in accord with one of the two sides. In legislative debate or a political campaign, there is no compromise. The audience votes yes or no, and the debater who takes the majority of votes takes everything. In this light, the viable idea is the force behind human action on all levels of communication. It may move a person, people, and nations. Its greatness is established when its influence extends beyond the population for which it is intended and beyond the time or generation in which it is first accepted.

In summary, human beings may be defined as makers of ideas who engage in both creative and critical processes, but a tendency toward one or the other might be used as a distinguishing characteristic to establish position in communication. Mature balance between creative expression and critical constraint moves human beings to action, singly and in groups, the results of which may ultimately be felt on much broader levels. But, when the individual does engage in interpersonal communication, he or she brings a total personality to bear on the event from the original inception of an idea to its face-to-face adaptation to an audience. The painter, composer, sculptor, writer, and architect, among others, must each rely on other people. In these cases, the receiver views, hears, or reads the product privately or, at best, in groups without the artist's presence. Seldom are creator and critic brought together; intermediaries, the musician, the actor, the carpenter, intervene. But in verbal lip-to-lobe communication personalities embody the source of power, and all faculties merge. In this way, interpersonal speech communication is the only art in which self-revelation is complete in all creative and critical processes, and it is this fact that makes people and their relative positions in this phenomenon of first importance.

PART II

PATTERNS IN SPEECH COMMUNICATION

Historical Perspective

Speech communication models,* it has been suggested, might be distinguished as 1) those in classical tradition, and 2) those in a more contemporary mode. The former gives emphasis to the speaker-speech relationship and the latter shifts the emphasis toward the listener-speech relationship. This distinction is acceptable when it is interpreted broadly. It loses some effect, however, when the implications of individual theorists, ancient and modern, are examined in detail. Cicero, for example, did not ignore the audience in communication; his suggestions to the speaker always carried the qualification that what is said must be considered in light of an audience's potential responses. In the same way, B. F. Skinner, as a modern case in point, does not neglect the speaker entirely since the forces responsible for the speaker's verbal behavior are always calculated by their impact upon him. The point to be made here, however, is that in Cicero's model of speech communication, the

---

*Traditionally, a speech communication model has represented a modelist's theoretical picture of important phenomena, elements and processes, common to all situations where the communication occurs. The difference between an element and a process, it should be explained, is comparable to the difference between a component and a function in a system. The chemical combination of oxygen and hydrogen to produce water helps to clarify this distinction. A process compares to the action of the "plus" and "equal" signs while an element corresponds to the elements of hydrogen and oxygen. A process, then, is a function. Elements are components which are modified by processes.

speaker is recognized as the source of the idea which unites persons in communication; B. F. Skinner's model of verbal behavior places the origin of the communication process in the speaker's environment, which includes the audience, and the speaker is clearly reacting to that audience when he speaks. In other words, Cicero's* starting point is the speaker, and the main ideas in his theory relate to the creative processes by which the speaker expresses himself; Skinner's starting point is the speaker's audience, and his primary concern involves the factors in an environment which determine the speaker's critical responses to them.

These two examples typify the extremes in speech communication models, but characteristically model builders have singled out one of the elements in the speech situation as the initiating force in communication and have related other elements and the processes in communication to this element. Even in instances where an attempt is made to accord equal stress to all elements, the modelist's starting point emerges in some way. This is patently true in verbal or linear models. In visual models, the upper, left-hand corner of a chart attracts first attention and

---

*Although there are substantial differences between the rhetorics of Aristotle and Cicero, one of the beliefs they shared was the view of rhetoric which hypothesized a popular audience and a responsible speaker. The speaker is distinctive in that he employs techniques to bring to the masses a clear, well-reasoned, and effective idea. Their rhetorics, then, dealt with the "authorship" of the speaker, his invention, arrangement, style, memory, and action. They further regarded the topics or commonplaces as residual elements of an education which speakers could carry with them and employ regardless of audience, occasion, and time. The speaker was conceived of as removed from but responsible to his audience. His ethic was an awareness of this responsibility, and his credibility depended on it.

what is seen there is consequently emphasized. Emphasis, however slight, offers a significant mark by which models of communication might be classified.

If the modelist attributes the first cause or source of an idea in communication to the communicator, the model tends toward the classical orientation where the speaker's persuasive purpose and his ability to achieve it are given prominence. This approach is comparable to what has been described as a model which rests on an intrapersonal philosophical base. An intrapersonal model attributes to the individual an inward appropriation of truth which transcends his perceptions of what occurs in the environment. In such a construct, the individual speaker attempts to modify the environment.

The opposite point of departure, which has been labelled extrapersonal, attributes stress to forces beyond the speaker. Members of an audience, for example, are credited with sufficient strength to infer from information alone and to guide or lead the speaker accordingly. Much of modern rhetoric minimizes the speaker's persuasive intent with an audience and points up the speaker's need to share information and to eliminate misinformation, the basis for intelligent decision making where the audience's views are primary. The speaker, then, is exhorted to search the environment for external proofs, unaltered by bias, which are mediated to audiences for their interpretation and use. Informational speaking, external proofs, and machines seem to go hand in hand with a modern or extrapersonal emphasis in speech communication models.

Designs

The most important practical implication of these two theories of communication involves the kinds of approach or design a speaker might use with audiences. If the speaker views an audience as weak and cooperative, the classical orientation makes sense.

The speaker tends to take the initiative and to express ideas in a directive way. Since most classical theories of speech communication were aimed at helping the recognized leader deal with the mass of commoners to be led, it is understandable that the speaker's authorship and the creative processes were accorded prominence in such theories. If people in the audience are viewed as strong but cooperative, as in contemporary communication models, the speaker tends to elicit their strength by raising questions, giving information, and seeking response, even guidance. Here the speaker is taking a non-directive approach by shifting responsibility for formulation of policy and specific actions to the audience or to the group the speaker represents. In a real sense, the development of contemporary models of speech communication awaited the rise of the common man and political democracy.

Designs might range, based on positions of people in communication, from the hard-sell, directive approach to the no-sale, non-directive approach in persuasion. The mid-point on the continuum might be termed the indirect, soft-sell design.

Just as the last five decades in American communication theory have signaled more emphasis on information and its destination, the audience, the last two decades in American public affairs have revealed public figures shifting more and more to non-directive designs in communication. Corporations "listen better." Politicians, reading unfavorable surveys of public opinion, either do not enter or withdraw from campaigns for public office. Parents have been seen more and heard less. Instead, children are being given a sympathetic ear, and they, like women, blacks, and other minority groups, seek independence from the father images traditional in American life. Authority figures are subject to more accountability by those over whom they have authority. Student-centered learning and client-centered therapy have achieved great popularity. In general, the presumption has been more and more assumed by the "outs," and the "ins" are now forced more and more to assume the burden of proof in protecting the status quo. Speakers are viewed less as leaders and more as mediators, representatives, and consultants. They, in turn, avoid the value judgments of the advocate.

Directive Designs

1. Dictation The general aversion to directive designs is in part due to revulsion against the behavior of the modern dictator, but there is a time and a place for such designs even when the speaker chooses to think of himself as open-minded and his community as democratic. In times of emergency, leaders may be forced to employ such designs. Certainly, the person whose friend does not see the car approaching and who shouts "Stop!" is using the appropriate design in light of the situation. The directive design, dictation, is best used, then, by speakers who rightly expect a recital of what has been said or compliance to orders given. The father/mother directing children or the military authority whose word is law best illustrate this design. Usually it takes relatively little time, and is followed by an exclamation point. Using the subject, the military capacity of the United States, a speech may be designed by dictation as follows:

    Introduction
        (Usually a simple allusion to the central idea sentence, CIS)

    Body
        CIS – THE UNITED STATES MUST INCREASE ITS MILITARY CAPACITY!

          I   The United States must increase its arms!
          II The United States must increase its manpower!

III   The United States must increase its
      military technology!

Conclusion
   (Usually a restatement of the CIS.)

   No matter which side of an issue a speaker supports, all dictatorial designs entail a positive statement of the proposition or CIS. It should also be noted that a positive statement of the CIS is implicit in directive designs generally. The proposition may make explicit the expansion of a given program, as in the example above, or it may represent decreasing, possibly eliminating a program. Even when a speaker dictates a cutback in a program, positive words like "consolidate," "retrench," and "streamline" might be used. Then, too, an affirmation of the opposite point of view may constitute the most appropriate wording. If the CIS represents a maintenance of the present level of a program, words like "limit," "balance," and "round off" might be employed. In all instances, however, the design remains the same, a bald statement of purpose detailed somewhat by main ideas. Notice that no supporting evidence for these ideas is offered.

   (2.) <u>Advocation</u>   The next directive design to be considered, advocacy, is slightly less directive because the speaker employs reasons and evidence to support the CIS. The reasons or arguments relate the central idea to values which the speaker presumes an audience will accept. A working definition of this persuasive design was best phrased by Aristotle when he suggested that the speaker's responsibility is to state his point and prove it. This design appears in almost all basic speech textbooks in connection with the speech to convince. Courts of law honor this approach regularly as lawyers argue the future of persons brought to trial by constructing reasons and evidence in case form. Nominees for public office speak to issues which clearly mark party differences, and these persons always argue just one side, their side, of such issues.

The difference between dictation and advocation comes down to the use of proof. In dictation none seems appropriate to the communicator, while reasons and evidence are indicated in advocation. Using the subject of the military capacity of the United States, an outline of a speech of advocacy might appear as follows.

    Introduction
        (Usually attention factors and immediate purpose are included.)

Body
    CIS - THE UNITED STATES SHOULD INCREASE ITS MILITARY CAPACITY.
     I Because: increased military capacity will offset external military threats.
       A Since: supporting evidence.
     II Because: increased military capacity will produce technological advances in all fields.
       A Since: supporting evidence
     III Because: increased military capacity will stimulate the American economy.
       A Since: supporting evidence.

Conclusion
    (Usually a summary and possibly an appeal are included.)

The speaker using advocacy employs reasons only to support propositions concerning the present formulation of thought and policy for the future. The speaker's use of reasons or deduction becomes highly suspect when the past is under consideration because deduction is superfluous in the analysis of what has already taken place. Induction, employing evidence based on fact, is the more substantial means of realistically establishing statements which can be verified about the past and should always be used when such a perspective is available. The facts of the past are potentially open to inspection, and the whys of such a situation are best put in the context of causation. It should also be noted that the causes of a situation can be transformed into reasons for future policy formation, but when that is true, they should be cast as reasons in support of a proposition about the future, not as causes of a past event. Causation will be taken up as a non-directive design, and the distinction between a cause and a reason will then be given additional treatment.

(3.) <u>Dualation</u> Although a directive technique, dualation or "two-sided advocacy" is more indirective than advocation because the speaker undertakes to view strong opposing arguments before committing him or herself to one specific side of the proposition under discussion. The communicator who uses dualation recognizes the opposing point of view by either briefly noting or, if choosing to be less directive, by devoting a main idea of the body of the speech to the other side of the case. When a speaker squeezes a point of view from great personal struggle, dualation is often an appropriate design. This is especially true when the audience faces the same struggle. While boarding a plane in Kansas City in 1961, a prominent religious leader was asked if he favored American nuclear disarmament. He replied that although Christian principles dictate against armament, even the Christian is forced to defend himself against enemies who threaten violence. Subsequent reasons, briefly stated, rounded out a clear-cut speech of dualation. A sample outline of such a speech might be as follows:

> Introduction
> (Usually attention factors and some information are included.)

Body
- I The argument that the United States has the present military capacity to make external military threats negligible has some merit.

  - A Because: the United States has sufficient military capacity to eliminate external military threats.
    - 1 Since: supporting evidence.
- II BUT, CIS - THE UNITED STATES SHOULD INCREASE ITS MILITARY CAPACITY.

  - A Because: increased military capacity will offset presently unknown external military threats.
    - 1 Since: supporting evidence.
  - B Because: increased military capacity will produce technological advances in all fields.
    - 1 Since: supporting evidence.
  - C Because: increased military capacity will stimulate the American economy.
    - 1 Since: supporting evidence

Conclusion
   (Usually a summary and possibly an appeal are included.)

Depending upon how directive a speaker wishes to be, the word "some" in main idea I might be altered. Indeed, the supporting evidence, possibly the reason, might be omitted. The omission of too much, however, shifts the first main idea to an introduction and the design to advocacy.

Non-Directive Designs

1. Interrogation At the other extreme of the continuum, the design of interrogation or inquiry corresponds to an open, honest question. This design implies a searching speaker who does not expect a pre-determined answer and marks exploration or experimentation in any field from politics to nuclear physics. Often, the most informed speaker employs available information to elaborate upon an important question which remains unanswered.

Using the same sample subject, the military capacity of the United States, a CIS might read as follows: How best can the United States improve the level of its military capacity? The word "improve" might be interpreted in many ways. The speaker could show some indirection, rather than complete non-direction, by using the words "strengthen" or "consolidate." The different assumptions behind the wording of questions can imply more direction or a complete lack of it in terms of the speaker's overall strategy. This design, for example, may constitute an introduction to a discussion or a conference, or an extended campaign over many hours, days, or months. The whole speech may, on the other hand, be intended simply to get and hold attention as a speech to interest. It should be noted that the question mark is at the core of humor, and the comic monologue might be thought of as the classic example of a non-directive design.

Typically, the question takes little time to express, and the speech of interrogation may be very brief. It does imply, as distinct from a brief speech of dictation, verbal response from the audience, and so, the occasion may involve a great deal of time in the long run. An outline of such a speech might look as follows:

> Introduction
> (Usually attention factors and background information are included.)

Body
- I How great is the United States' military capacity?
- II How great should the United States' military capacity be?
- III How can the United States best bring what its military is to what it should be?
- CIS HOW BEST CAN THE UNITED STATES IMPROVE THE LEVEL OF ITS MILITARY CAPACITY?

Conclusion
    (Usually a summary and raising of questions are included.)

(2.) Description   The design closest to the non-directive extreme of interrogation is description. This design compares closely to what is more generally understood as the speech to inform. The dilemma as to whether or not information is persuasive answers itself in terms of the construct drawn here. Explication is non-directive in design, but it is potentially persuasive. An objective description, demonstration, or definition, all of which are explicatory to some degree, involve non-direction since no sale or point of view is either consciously or immediately sought. An audience, however, may infer from information a point of view and, in some cases, a kind of behavior. In strategic situations, information may be required before a speaker can move to more directive approaches. All designs are persuasive in nature, but some are less obviously persuasive than others. Such is the case with description.

An example of description involving American military capacity follows:

Introduction
    (Usually attention factors are included in extended form, and there may be some allusion to the CIS.)

Body
- I The United States has curtailed its development of arms technology.
   - A As seen in: supporting materials.
- II The United States has decreased its manpower quotas.
   - A As seen in: supporting materials.
- III The United States has lost some military bases around the world.
   - A As seen in: supporting materials.

CIS – THE UNITED STATES' MILITARY CAPACITY HAS DIMINISHED IN RECENT YEARS.

Conclusion
   (Usually a summary, a clear statement of the CIS, and the raising of questions, are included.)

3. <u>Causation</u> Causation, less non-directive than description, is a design based upon cause-effect relationships. Sorting through the whys of a situation for an audience is less non-directive or more indirective than description because a discussion of causes or effects shifts the communicator closer to a suggestion of value judgment or a specific point of view toward the subject discussed. When a form of government, for example, is objectively described, there may be no implication that the speaker has a point of view concerning it. But when the speaker discusses causes for its occurrence, these causes may have been thought of at one point in time as reasons for accepting it. An audience's inferential leap from causes to reasons is often automatic. These causes, then, whether interpreted objectively or subjectively mark a shift toward indirection, away from the no-sale position of description.

Notice the difference between the following example of causation and the example given earlier of advocacy.

Introduction
    (Usually attention factors, background information, and, possibly, allusion to the CIS are included.)

Body
- I Americans have lost interest in the external military threats to the United States.
  - A As seen in: supporting materials.
- II Americans have lost interest in the development of advanced military technology.
  - A As seen in: supporting materials.
- III Americans have become more interested in domestic issues.
  - A As seen in: supporting materials.

CIS – THE DIMINISHED MILITARY CAPACITY OF THE UNITED STATES IS DUE TO THE CHANGE IN INTERESTS OF AMERICANS.

Conclusion
    (Usually a summary of causes, perhaps reference to the effects of the situation, and the raising of questions are included.)

Causation, then, may be thought of as the contemporary approach to a given situation in an attempt to understand the whys of what is, as distinct from the reasons for what should be. A special concern for reasons which has been associated with the classical approach to communication and which forms the basis of a directive approach in persuasion is implicit in treating a subject as it should, could, or would be. Reasons are most appropriate in supporting plans for the future; causes are most appropriate in analyzing events of the past. When a speaker speaks of the future in terms of causes, or reasons deductively about the past, that person is, in the first case, confusing scientific analysis with crystal ball gazing and, in the second case, using artistic deduction where scientific induction is the more certain method. The past is open to a scientific analysis of evidence. The future is not, and the speaker who plans for the future must reason on the basis of probabilities which entails the logical synthesis of ideas.

Reasons, after the fact, become causes, and, by the same token, all apparent causes before the fact must be recognized as possible reasons. Any other interpretation is not only misleading, but may lead to the insanity of being certain about the future, or writing the past as it should or could have been, rather than as it was.

Indirective Designs

Ranged between these two kinds of designs, the directive and the non-directive, stand several designs which might be thought of as indirective in nature. These designs are the most sophisticated and the most productive of persuasive designs. They represent positions which adults take toward each other when equality is assumed, and they embody combinations of the non-directive and directive designs.

Important enough to be repeated, the distinction between design and disposition is the difference between the division of a communique into subordinate units and the tactical synthesis of these units for the purpose of persuasion. In other words, disposition in speech implies classification or the grouping of supporting materials around ideas selected by the speaker as the most salient features of the central idea while the tactical placement of these units of main ideas denotes design. It should also be reiterated that design may embody either a communicator's ultimate goal or a compromise between the long range purpose and the limitations imposed upon the situation by the audience's frame of reference. Speakers, then, employ design as an end

A SPECTRUM OF COMMUNICATIVE DESIGN

"SOFT-SELL" INDIRECTION

"NO-SALE" NON-DIRECTION			"HARD-SELL" DIRECTION
	FATHER	ULTRA VIOLET	
		VIOLET	UNCLE
	UNCLE	INDIGO	
		BLUE	BROTHER
	BROTHER	GREEN	
		YELLOW	
	NEPHEW	ORANGE	
		RED	NEPHEW
	SON	INFRARED	

Lower labels: SON — NEPHEW — BROTHER — UNCLE — FATHER

INTERROGATION
DESCRIPTION
CAUSATION
PARASTATION
COALATION
PROBLEMATION
DUALATION
ADVOCATION
DICTATION

SPEECH

point in thinking or as a means to an end.

(1.) **Parastation**. A consideration of the causes of a given situation may result in honest confusion and ambivalence. Two inimical statements may both be accepted as valid. Therefore, many answers to vital questions are paradoxical in nature. Incorporating paradox into the design of a message is best thought of as an indirective approach, but the indirective design closest to non-direction. For clarity's sake, it might be viewed as the design located between causation and the very middle of the continuum of persuasive designs, i.e., coalation.

Communicators in the American tradition often avoid this design because it smacks too much of equivocation in a country where people are accustomed to either-or thinking. A foot in both camps is viewed by many as slipshod preparation for public office. Consequently, this design is completely neglected by writers of speech textbooks. However, it is the best design available for the communicator who truly feels that two diametrically opposed points of view or two contradictory interpretations of the facts should both be presented as valid. Parastation or stating both sides of a case may in fact represent the only honest approach a speaker can take. An example of parastation in American public speaking is found in Booker T. Washington's Atlanta Exposition Address where he likened the black's desires to the hand and fingers. His people, he said, wanted to be a part of the whole, the hand, where economic matters were concerned, but separate, like the fingers, in social affairs. Nikita Kruschev seemed to recognize the necessity of paradox in the real world, that two different ways of life can exist side by side, when he used parastation to design his ideas in support of co-existence. Although his long term strategy appeared to be the hard-sell of communism, his tactic or design was indirect. A prominent educator assessed the comparative merits of specializa-

tion and generalization in education and resolved
the dilemma by indicating that modern education
needs more of both.

There are basically two kinds of parastation.
One involves fact; the other, belief. In both cases,
however, the acceptance of contradiction is implicit.
If the facts of a matter are contradictory, both
sides might be presented as follows:

> Introduction
>   (Usually attention factors, background
>   information, and, possibly, allusion to
>   indecision are included.)
>
> Body
> I The United States' military capacity
>   is especially strong in military
>   technology.
>   A As seen in: supporting materials.
> II The United States' military capacity
>   is especially weak in military
>   resources.
>   A There is weakness in manpower.
>   1 As seen in: supporting materials.
>   B There is weakness in arms.
>   1 As seen in: supporting materials.
> III CIS - THE MILITARY CAPACITY OF THE
>   UNITED STATES IS A MIXTURE OF STRENGTH
>   AND WEAKNESS.
>   A As seen in: above main ideas and
>   supporting materials.
>
> Conclusion
>   (Usually a summary, an indication of
>   ambivalence, and a raising of questions
>   are included.)

When a speaker's beliefs are contradictory,
regardless of the facts, parastation still comes
into play. Here the speaker accepts the advantages
and/or disadvantages of both sides of the proposition. This stance compares to the debater's or

lawyer's brief where both sides of the point at issue are outlined and documented. The main ideas of such a presentation might be designed as follows:

Introduction
    (Usually attention factors, background information, and, possibly, allusion to indecision are included.)

Body
  I An increase in military capacity would benefit the United States.
    A Because: increased military capacity will offset presently unknown external military threats.
      1 Since: supporting evidence.
    B Because: increased military capacity will produce technological advances in all fields.
      1 Since: supporting evidence.
  II A curtailment of military capacity would benefit the United States.
    A Because: the United States has sufficient military capacity to eliminate external military threats.
      1 Since: supporting evidence.
    B Because: the United States' domestic problems command the use of available resources.
  III CIS - THE BENEFITS OF INCREASING AND CURTAILING THE MILITARY CAPACITY OF THE UNITED STATES ARE EQUALLY VALID.
    A Because: above reasons and evidence are equally valid.

Conclusion
    (Usually a summary, an indication of ambivalence, and a raising of questions are included.)

Notice that in this indirective design, the
kind of parastation based upon belief, another subject has been introduced. There has been an initial
attempt made to balance the subject of military
capacity with domestic or non-military concerns. At
the center of the continuum of persuasive design
another continuum representing another subject must
be recognized. That is, the kinds of directive and
non-directive designs which have been used in regard to military capacity of the United States might
have been used in regard to a specific domestic subject like poverty in the United States. These two
continua of design might meet, criss-crossing at
their mid-points. When a domestic or non-military
concern enters into a discussion of military concerns, as inevitably it will if American policy in
general is considered, indirective designs permit
the consideration of both subjects in one speech.

At the point where indirection becomes the
approach most appropriate to the speaker, audience,
and subject, other subjects, then, must be considered
to admit the complexities of thinking necessary in
treating involved problems that exist in the real-life world. Priorities which are very real in
managing anything from a home to a national foreign
policy, are based on a comparison and mixing of subjects initially thought to be unrelated. The concept of cost-benefits exemplifies this principle
clearly. When costs are balanced off against
benefits, two subjects, money and other values, are
joined to achieve the right mix: ultimately the
most benefit for the least cost, but for the moment,
the right benefit with the right cost. Great cost
and great benefit might be two main ideas in parastation. An illustration, based on the example
used throughout this treatment of design follows:

>Introduction
>>(Usually attention factors, background
information, and, possibly, allusion
to indecision are included.)

Body
- I An increase in military capacity would benefit the United States.
  - A Because: increased military capacity will offset presently unknown external military threats.
    - 1 Since: supporting evidence
  - B Because: increased military capacity will produce technological advances in all fields.
    - 1 Since: supporting evidence.
- II An increase in support of domestic poverty areas would benefit the United States.
  - A Because: increased support will improve the economic condition of persons in poverty areas.
    - 1 Since: supporting evidence
  - B Because: increased support will create job opportunities generally.
- III CIS - BENEFITS WILL ACCRUE FROM BOTH INCREASED MILITARY CAPACITY AND INCREASED SUPPORT OF DOMESTIC POVERTY AREAS.
  - A Because: above reasons and evidence are all valid.

Conclusion
   (Usually a summary, an indication of ambivalence, and a raising of questions are included.)

Before making the logical move to coalation, it is necessary to move to the directive side of indirection to consider problemation. It will become apparent that it is just as logical to move to coalation from problemation as it is from parastation. Both problemation and parastation bring

the communicator to the most difficult but the most
rewarding design in the continuum of design, coalation, a synthesis or blend of two or more subjects
in one idea.

2. <u>Problemation</u> This design permits the
speaker to be both non-directive and directive in
one speech. A speaker viewing the past, defining,
and diagnosing a problem, is initially employing
designs which have been discussed as non-directive.
As the speaker moves into the answer to the problem,
suggestions about the future are made and the position of the advocate is assumed. This suits the
communicator who wishes to prepare his audience
more fully for his views. In dictation, advocation, and dualation, the problem is implied in the
introduction of the speech. But problemation permits the speaker to be more indirect, to postpone
a point of view until the audience's need for an
answer to a given problem has been analyzed. The
body of most sales talks to general audiences includes a main idea concerning the customer's problem.
In sales talks, the salesman sows the seeds of an
answer as he limits and analyzes the problem. The
audience is prepared by indirection to accept a plan
for solving the problem, and often the speaker with-
holds a statement of the central idea sentence until
the plan becomes apparent.

Were it not for the fact that this design
has become common currency in textbooks in many
fields where communication is considered, it might
be viewed as a combination of many designs. It has
achieved a status which demands its recognition,
however, as an individual design in and of itself.
The standard form of this design follows:

    Introduction
        (Usually attention factors, definitions,
           and historical background are included.)

Body
- I The military capacity of the United States is inadequate.
  - A Due to: a slowdown of American military technological advances.
    - 1 As seen in: supporting materials.
  - B Due to: a cutback in American conventional military forces.
    - 1 As seen in: Supporting materials.
- II CIS – THE UNITED STATES SHOULD INSTITUTE A PROGRAM OF INCREASED MILITARY CAPACITY (P.I.M.C.).
  - A Because: P.I.M.C. is desirable
    - 1 Because: it will activate American military technological advances.
      - a Since: supporting evidence.
    - 2. Because: it will strengthen American conventional military forces.
      - a Since: supporting evidence.
  - B Because: P.I.M.C. is practicable.
    - 1 Because: The United States has the necessary technological knowledge.
      - a Since: supporting evidence.
    - 2 Because: the United States has the necessary financial resources.
      - a Since: supporting evidence.

Conclusion
(Usually a summary, appeal, and, possibly, the raising of questions are included.)

When an existing situation is labelled inadequate or in some way deficient, as in the first main idea of the above illustration, that labelling constitutes a critical reaction or a non-directive tactic in persuasion. The only justification for making the first main idea in problemation the sum total of a presentation is the analysis of a situation, and this would result in a nondirective approach. What makes problemation an indirective-directive approach is the second main idea which incorporates a positive plan to correct a situation which is seen as weak and potentially dangerous. If speakers, for example, who assume an affirmative stance in debate do not follow their criticism of the status quo with a positive suggestion for the future, they remain ineffective advocates. As informants, however, their interpretations may be accurate and astute.

It is also noted in the above illustration that an abbreviation of the plan has been suggested. Usually plans or projects recommended as policy guides are given shorthand titles. Bills in Congress are often named after the person introducing them. Then, too, initials are employed as T.V.A., N.O.W., and the example given here, P.I.M.C. Abbreviated mottoes are also used, e.g., New Deal, Great Society, and Common Cause.

As in the case of any directive design, the plan in problemation can range all the way from expansion of a program, as in the above example, to consolidation, from the strongest to the weakest affirmative positions. Re-establishing or maintaining a program represents a weaker, but relatively strong position. Modifying or revamping a program is a relatively weak position, and diminishing by consolidation is the weakest position. The elimination of a program would be a negative approach and would appropriately serve either as the first main idea in a speech of problemation or the CIS in a more non-directive approach such as explication or causation.

The speaker, as in the case of parastation, faces situations where two or more subjects must be

considered in developing a program to provide the
most benefit for the most people. This may mean that
one part or several of a nation's, or organization's,
or family's, or group's needs might have to be neglected. In the process of solving one problem, a
speaker may absolve himself of solving a second or
third problem. The existence of a problem does not
constitute a reason for solving it. The problem may
not receive the highest or higher priority in which
case it may be given relatively little time and
effort. Cutting back on the support of one need in
order to answer another usually appears in the second
main idea of problemation under the stock issue of
practicability as follows:

 Introduction
  (Usually attention factors, definitions,
   and historical background are included.)

 Body
  I The military capacity of the United
   States is inadequate.
   A Due to: a slowdown of American
     military technological
     advances.
    1 As seen in: supporting materials.
   B Due to: a cutback in American con-
     ventional military forces.
    1 As seen in: supporting materials.
  II CIS – DESPITE DOMESTIC NEEDS, THE
   UNITED STATES SHOULD INSTITUTE A
   PROGRAM OF INCREASED MILITARY CAPA-
   CITY (P.I.M.C.).
   A Because: P.I.M.C. is desirable.
    1 Because: it will activate American
     military technological
     advances.
     a Since: supporting evidence.
    2 Because: it will strengthen
     American conventional
     military forces.

             a Since: supporting evidence.
          B Because: if domestic needs are post-
                    poned, P.I.M.C. is practi-
                    cable.
             1 Because: domestic needs can be
                       postponed.
                a Since: supporting evidence
             2 Because: the United States has
                       the resources to meet the
                       cost of P.I.M.C.
                b Since: supporting evidence.

     Conclusion
          (Usually a summary, appeal, and possibly,
          the raising of questions are included.)

     Notice that in this design, priorities have
been established. P.I.M.C. is thought to be an
answer to a more significant problem requiring an
immediate answer. Other needs, such as poverty areas
on the domestic front, have been considered of less
significance and, consequently, have not been an-
swered. Their postponement may be temporary or
permanent, depending upon the importance attached
to them by the speaker.

     A third form of problemation incorporates
more than one need in the first main idea, e.g., the
weakness of American military capacity and the poverty
of certain areas in the United States. The second
main idea might represent the speaker's attempt to
provide a mechanism or plan whereby both problems are
treated in greater detail. The complexity of problems
facing the modern executive may require an intermedi-
ate step between the recognition of the problems and
their solution. Before a program, then, which meets
two or many needs can be devised, more formal consideration may be required. An example of such a
design follows:

     Introduction
          (Usually attention factors, definitions,
          and historical background are included.)

Body
- I The United States faces two (or more) important problems.
  - A Due to: the inadequacies of American military capacity.
    - 1 As seen in: supporting materials.
  - B Due to: the poverty of certain areas in the United States.
    - 1 As seen in: supporting materials.

- II CIS - A BOARD INCLUDING REPRESENTATION FROM THE MILITARY, CONGRESS, LABOR AND INDUSTRY SHOULD BE ESTABLISHED TO DEVELOP A PROGRAM WHICH WILL MEET THESE TWO NEEDS.
  - A Because: such a board would include knowledgeable people from many areas.
    - 1 Since: supporting evidence.
  - B Because: such a board would have the potential to devise a practicable answer to two very important needs.
    - 1 Since: supporting evidence.

Conclusion
(Usually a summary, appeal, and, possibly, the raising of questions are included.)

This third form of problemation, as in the case of parastation, has carried the speaker's thoughts to the brink of coalation. This time, however, the speaker has approached from the directive side of the continuum. While both parastation and problemation represent combinations of the nondirective and directive designs, it is at the point of coalation that these designs become one. At the same time that coalation synthesizes designs, it also synthesizes apparently contradictory or initially unrelated problems or subject areas. A domestic problem and a foreign affairs problem may be juxtapositioned in such a way as to lead to one plan which will treat both problems.

(3.) Coalation Coalation differs from parastation and problemation as a blend is distinct from a combination. Coalation is to gray as both parastation and problemation are to black and white. Henry Grady, Abraham Lincoln, and the great compromisers prior to the Civil War represented in their crowning moments examples of communicators mediating two divergent points of view. The attempt was made by the compromisers to bring the North and South into a peace-conducive relationship by accepting new territories as States on the basis of equal distribution between slave and non-slave States. The doctrine of equal time for political parties on national television is a modern example of this design. This kind of plan illustrates the first type of coalation available to the communicator, particularly the communicator whose role is that of mediator or conference leader. The principle is equal distribution, and the practice involves a neutral acceptance of both the strengths and weaknesses of two diametrically opposed points of view as they are blended in one plan or package. The object is to incorporate more of the advantages and less of the disadvantages of both plans or objects into the final product. An example of this type of coalation, using the subjects already treated in other illustrations of design, follows:

    Introduction
        (Usually attention factors, definitions, and historical background are included.)

    Body
      I There are domestic strengths and weaknesses in the United States.
         A Due to: strengths in the economy.
           1 As seen in: supporting materials.
         B Due to: weaknesses in the economy.
           1 As seen in: supporting materials.
      II There are military strengths and weaknesses in the United States.
         A Due to: strengths in the military.
           1 As seen in: supporting materials.

　　　　　B Due to: weaknesses in the military
　　　　　　　1 As seen in: supporting materials.
　　　III　CIS - A PLAN OF EQUAL DISTRIBUTION OF
　　　　　RESOURCES WILL MODERATELY INCREASE THE
　　　　　STRENGTHS AND MODERATELY DIMINISH THE
　　　　　WEAKNESSES IN BOTH MILITARY CAPACITY
　　　　　AND DOMESTIC STABILITY.
　　　　　A Because: Both the military and do-
　　　　　　　　　　　mestic are equally important.
　　　　　　　1 Since: supporting evidence.
　　　　　B Because: Equal distribution is prac-
　　　　　　　　　　　ticable
　　　　　　　1 Since: supporting evidence.

　　Conclusion
　　　　(Usually a summary is included.)

　　　This design represents a four-way split of
efforts and resources over both the strengths and
weaknesses of both the military and domestic subject
areas. The striking strengths and weaknesses in both
areas are mitigated as an equal distribution of resources is incorporated into a practical plan for
dealing with two or more problem situations. It must
be remembered, however, as strengths and weaknesses
are joined to ameliorate both, the blend is such that
the identities of the opposites which are combined
are submerged in the development of the new identity.
If the solutions of military and domestic needs are
easily identified as separate, the coalation is not
achieved. The design remains either parastation or
problemation. Marriage, for example, involves both
parastation and coalation. Viewed from within, the
home is a combination of opposites (parastation).
Individual differences are submerged (coalation)
when the family is viewed by an outsider. The child
of husband and wife represents coalation in its
purest state because the identities of the opposites
are totally lost in their synthesis.

　　　Imagine a Kansas City high school senior in
doubt about choice of colleges. The student con-
siders both Missouri University and National College. M. U. is relatively large, cosmopolitan, and

away from home. National College is by comparison
small, parochial, and located in his hometown.
Representatives from both the college and the university might attempt persuasion by advocacy. A
friend might suggest parastation, National College
for the first two years and M. U. for the last two
years. A representative from a third institution,
Central Missouri State College, employing coalation,
might point out that C.M.S.C. is middle-sized,
slightly cosmopolitan, and some small distance from
home. The advantages (and disadvantages, it should
be noted) of both extremes are mixed in one entity.
The advantages of such a blend are emphasized, the
positive approach being preferable to the negative
in human motivation.

The second kind of coalation centers on a
package plan aimed at strengthening the weaknesses
in two or more different areas or entities. Such a
design would work toward rectifying weaknesses without giving immediate attention to strengths. This
design is comparable to compromise in a situation
where the needs of both sides in a dispute, management and labor, for example, are treated with the
thought that strengths will take care of themselves
or, perhaps, even be increased by the action to correct weaknesses. In negotiations, labor might believe its greatest need is better working conditions.
Management might concede that point in order to receive reciprocal concessions in another area. If
the company's profits have fallen and this is viewed
as a pressing weakness, management may well seek preference in the matter of wage. Under these circumstances, a mediator might design an idea by coalation,
meeting the respective needs of both parties through
a plan encompassing better working conditions and
lower wage increases. The principle here is reciprocity.

Notice in the following example how the
special needs on the domestic and military fronts
are pinpointed and treated in one idea. This treat-

ment is offered for illustrative purposes only; it is not necessarily "the" answer.

>   Introduction
>   (Usually attention factors, definitions, and historical background are included.)
>
>   Body
>   I The domestic economy in the United States has severe weaknesses.
>   A Due to: the poverty levels of existence in some areas of the population.
>   1 As seen in: supporting materials.
>   II The American military capacity has severe weaknesses.
>   A Due to: the lack of conventional military resources.
>   1 As seen in: supporting materials.
>   III CIS - MILITARY BASES/FACTORIES SHOULD BE BUILT IN AND/OR SHIFTED TO POVERTY AREAS IN THE UNITED STATES.
>   A Because: military bases/factories would revitalize the economy of poverty areas.
>   1 Since: supporting evidence.
>   B Because: military bases/factories would produce needed men and materials for national security.
>
>   Conclusion
>   (Usually a summary is included.)

A third kind of coalation attempts to exercise and increase the strengths in one area or product to eliminate the weaknesses in another, and vice versa. In chess, this kind of design, based on synthesis, would compare to the move which is strong both offensively and defensively. It is based on the principle of total synthesis of benefits in which all key problems are solved. In the first two types of coalation where, in the first case, equal distribution and, in the second, reciprocity (a trading of needs) are suggested, the result involves resolution of the immediate problems faced. Complete solution is not achieved, and the parties involved are not expected to be completely satisfied. Due to any number of causes, these may be the only designs or tactics available to the communicator. In the third type of coalation, however, an attempt is made to eliminate weaknesses and maximize strengths in two or more problem areas simultaneously. This design results in one plan or entity devoid of the weaknesses but incorporating the strengths of its own originating components or sources.

Arriving at a plan which accomplishes such a task is intellectually the most demanding process in persuasive design. Nevertheless, the advantages are worth the difficulties because this design, once completed, represents the creative cutting edge in the expansion and progress of a democratic society. Solving complicated problems, social or otherwise, should be the most highly prized of human activities, and inventors, statesmen, researchers, and leaders generally, whose thoughtful answers to hard problems where a synthesis of areas of knowledge has led to real solutions, should be rewarded as the most gifted citizens of a democracy.

While an answer to military and domestic weaknesses which would accomplish what is suggested in this last type of coalation is not attempted here, illustration of the design is essential. An intimation of what is involved follows:

Introduction
(Usually attention factors, definitions, and historical background are included.)

Body
I There are special strengths in the American domestic economy and American military capacity.

    A Due to: the strengths of management and production abilities of American industry.
      1 As seen in: supporting materials.
    B Due to: the strengths of technology and technologists of the American military.
      1 As seen in: supporting materials.
II There are special weaknesses in the American domestic economy and American military capacity.
    A Due to: the observed unemployment levels in American proverty areas.
      1 As seen in: supporting materials.
    B Due to: the observed low levels of men and materials in the American military.
III CIS - A NATIONAL DOMESTIC PEACE/DEFENSE CORPS MADE UP OF SOLDIERS AND UNEMPLOYED CIVILIANS SHOULD BE FORMED UNDER THE COMBINED LEADERSHIP OF INDUSTRIAL MANAGERS AND MILITARY TECHNOLOGISTS.
    A Because: such a corps would improve, by construction and beautification, living conditions in the United States.
      1 Since: supporting evidence
    B Because: such a corps would improve, by construction and training, the military defenses of the United States.
      1 Since: supporting evidence.
    C Because: such a corps would provide employment for the unemployed and would acquaint them with disciplines needed by the military in national emergencies.
      1 Since: supporting evidence.

          D Because: such a corps would provide
                    exercise for the talents of
                    civilian and military per-
                    sons in both peaceful and
                    defensive activities.
            1 Since: supporting evidence.

   Conclusion
      (Usually a summary is included.)

     All forms of coalation attempt a synthesis of
two or more apparently distinct, if not contradictory,
entities as well as a synthesis of non-directive and
directive approaches in persuasion. Coalation as a
design is different from parastation and problemation in more than academic ways. For hard-minded
salesmen, for example, this distinction means the
difference between basing a sales campaign on an individually tailored answer to a customer's problem
(problemation), the idea of two cars in the garage,
one for long trips and the other for town driving
(parastation), and the synthesis of both in one
(coalation), a compact large enough for turnpikes
and small enough to spike the turns around home.

     It should be noted, too, the distinctions
between the various types of coalation depend in
part on time. An equal distribution of resources,
time, energy, etc. is usually based on past policies.
Reciprocity builds on the immediacy of present needs.
Ideal synthesis implies a view to the future through
long-term planning.

     While these designs have been discussed as
separate entities, they lend themselves to many
combinations. In fact, they appear most often in
the real-life world of communication in combination.
This is probably due to the heterogeneity of listeners and to the general lack of knowledge of persuasive design. Communicators tend to follow the
laws of nature, and, just as pure primary colors are
seldom found in nature, so pure persuasive designs

are rarely heard in the personal and platform efforts of speakers who respond to their listeners. Yet, as a prism separates the colors of the rainbow, analysis can serve to isolate a communicator's primary design even when it blankets many other less prominent and different designs. Such analysis permits the consideration of the very practical questions about the relationship of designs or patterns to people.

Part III attempts to clarify this relationship. How are patterns best related to people in the practical sense to achieve communication? Which designs are most communicative with which people? Practical techniques in delivery are also discussed.

PART III

PRACTICE IN SPEECH COMMUNICATION

The sometimes difficult and time-consuming processes of understanding people and patterns in speech communication find justification in the speaker's practical application of such an understanding to help others cooperate as equals in support of worthwhile ideas. These aims, equality and cooperation, are sought simultaneously; neither should be neglected at the expense of the other. If one has to be sacrificed, however, equality should be maintained at the cost of cooperation.

Where adults are concerned, the kind of cooperation or acceptance achieved at the cost of equality is the least productive both in terms of the relationship itself and the ideas which result, In the extreme, an effort to establish equality may terminate a relationship, but that remains a better alternative than the other extreme, slavery or cooperation at any cost. Inequality eventually causes disruption and a broken relationship in any event. Equality in relationships also offers greater value than cooperation because a competition between equals produces more ideas of value than a coopertive acceptance of a leader by followers. There is greater possibility of productive discussion between equals. When a choice is necessary, then, equality is of greater importance to the persuader. Practical communication, however, should achieve both ends, and relating the appropriate pattern to the appropriate person, small group, or large group of people is aimed at performing this dual function.

The practical speaker first recognizes the relative positions of others to him or herself as ideas of common interest are shared. Who is the subordinate or have-not? Who is the superior or have? How close are persons in communication to a position of equality, equal to equal? In short, who are the strong, and who are the weak?

Dimensions of Strength/Weakness

In answering questions concerning relative position in communication, the speaker must engage in what traditionally has been called audience analysis. Audiences on the interpersonal level may range in size from one individual to as many as possible within unaided earshot of the speaker. This maximum number varies according to the speaker's voice, circumstances in the environment, and the keenness of hearing in members of the audience. Some unusual interpersonal situations may include hundreds of auditors.

Individual Dimensions

Although cultural and social influences are important even in very small group interaction, auditors are individuals first, and the communicator must recognize them as such when an attempt is made to gauge dimensions of strength/weakness. The key questions in an analysis of any one person are as follows:* How much does a person know about the idea under discussion? How emotionally stable is a person toward the idea? How strongly does a person hold what beliefs toward the idea? And how consistently active is a person in support of beliefs, feelings, and knowledge?

1. <u>Knowledge</u> Francis Bacon's statement to the effect that knowledge is power has a universal following. The more one knows, the stronger he or she is. In terms of personality construct developed in Part I,

---

*These primary dimensions of an audience were first classified in this fashion for the author by Franklin H. Knower in a graduate seminar at the Ohio State University.

a lack of knowledge is associated with the subordinate position in persuasion; an increase in knowledge relative to others leads in direct proportion to an increase in strength. The superior position in persuasion evolves in part from superior knowledge. When two people in communication have achieved approximately the same amount of knowledge, an equal to equal relationship develops naturally.

In cases where one person decides to play a game, recognition of position becomes tenuous; an admission of weakness is sometimes extremely difficult, but it is the only means by which an honest equality can eventually be achieved. Too often, speakers bamboozle listeners into feigning a knowledge which they do not really possess, and under these circumstances, changes which are supposed to result either in the individual's understanding or in the development of the relationship simply do not happen, despite appearances.

    2. _Interest_ The ability to demonstrate a consistently deep-seated concern is almost always aligned with personal strength. Inability to concentrate is a sign of weakness. For example, little children lack powers of concentration and often require dramatic, even shocking, displays to sustain interest. Indeed, a short attention span is never effective in complicated situations which demand time and intense scrutiny. These situations call for strength of concentration, and adults with a reasonably wide variety of concerns are seldom expected to need constant reminders that the idea being discussed is interesting. Of course, interest usually goes hand in hand with knowledge. Except in unusual circumstances, the more knowledge of a subject a person has, the more intense the interest. Some listeners, unfortunately, have cultivated a "sincere" listening style which they apply to all speakers, and, too frequently, this leads to game behavior in what should be a real-life stiuation. It almost goes without saying that speakers

should not purposely set out to be dull.

3. <u>Emotional Stability</u> Another indication of strength involves the individual's ability to remain stable where undue emotional involvement and mental lapses are likely. The stronger the person, the less susceptible that person is to tears, shock, and dazed bewilderment, reactions regularly expected of children. Adapting to a world of problems in any culture, particularly where change is encouraged, makes personal stability difficult, but when the individual ceases to be overly disturbed by adjustment, he or she has achieved a level of strength necessary to function in such a world and is accorded adult status. While few people deny the need for a good, honest cry occasionally, the individual who seeks strength, must avoid such displays.

4. <u>Belief</u> Well-supported and strongly held beliefs have been associated consistently with strength. The superior position in communication demands of the individual a commitment to some, if not many, clearly defined beliefs. Persons who adhere to long-term beliefs, when it may be more expedient to revise or abandon them, are viewed as especially strong in a communicative relationship. Too often, being open-minded is accepted as a sign of strength, when it is actually a method for discarding beliefs or retreating in the face of a pressure situation. Where an honestly open-minded approach is taken, it is consonant with childlike investigation and should be viewed as a position of weakness. Again, this is not to say that weakness in communication is always to be avoided.

It should be noted in each of these primary dimensions that the listener's strength or weakness is not necessarily good or bad. An honest recognition of weakness may be conducive to equality and better ideas. Ignorance, boredom, instability, inconsistent or weakly-held beliefs, and random behavior all need to be recognized before change toward strength can occur.

5. _Activity_ High energy levels and a consistent pattern of behavior are also considered characteristic of the strong person. In other words, when a person can be relied upon to act energetically in a certain way under certain circumstances, the Western tradition labels that person as strong. Conversely, the person who is unpredictable and/or indolent is usually considered unreliable and, therefore, weak. Adult equality and cooperation in relationships depend upon consistency of behavior, and the fact that the son or daughter in a family relationship is relatively dependent and unreliable makes the parent's protective position necessary.

Social Influences

While individual characteristics are of first concern, the immediate social environment is also important in determining strength and weakness in communication because the size of the group determines in part its strength; the larger the group, the stronger. Also, the characteristics of individuals are modified by relationships within social groupings. Individuals play many roles. They may relate socially as peacemakers, jokesters, activity leaders, gossip carriers, and so on. One specific role, however, is of special concern to the persuader in recognizing strength and weakness. The person in a social grouping who has the most influence is the opinion leader. These people have been defined as persons who are especially effective listeners and speakers.

Opinion leaders are not to be confused with thought leaders. The thought leader is an easily recognized group leader. He or she holds high office within a society or organization and has influence which extends vertically or perpendicularly to all lower levels within the organization. The opinion leader, however, operates along horizontal lines at one given level within the group. The thought leader's influence is reinforced by parental authority. The opinion leader relates to others on the basis of adult equality, the first among equals. The opinion leader seldom, if ever, actually leads the group, gives speeches, or holds office. He or she may never speak formally in group meetings, and, as a result, is a relatively difficult person to isolate and observe.

The tendency for opinion leaders to conceal their influence has led students of communication to ignore them. While these people are hard to identify, personality characteristics common to opinion leaders are activity, sensitivity, and a willingness to communicate informally. Opinion leaders are more gregarious than others. They are members of many volunteer organizations, but do not hold offices. They are more venturesome in their approach to new ideas. They tend to linger after meetings to discuss with others the practical implications of business completed during the formalities of the meeting itself. Consequently, they are the people most imitated and the people whose approval is most often sought. Of course, these characteristics relate directly to individual characteristics already described as indicative of strength.

The practical methods of determining who opinion leaders are evolve logically from the persuader's knowledge of their distinguishing characteristics. Who in a group, for example, is sought out for advice? Who has influenced others in the group? Answers to these questions lead to or locate the opinion leader, and once found, this person can be invaluable to the persuader who is in doubt about his or her position relative to the group. Opinion leaders serve best in this way: they are indicators of general group or audience response. To center in on the opinion leader, to speak only to him or her in public is usually ill-advised because the group makes its own opinion leaders, and when they become so identified with the persuader that they are no longer thought of as group members, they are no

longer influential as opinion leaders. They become
associated with the perpendicular lines of authority
and assume roles as thought leaders. Any public display, then, of special concern for opinion leaders
is best avoided lest their value as shorthand versions
of reading an audience is lost.

Cultural Background

The cultural backgrounds of others are of
special concern to the communicator because each
listener has internalized to some extent the critical
standards of his or her cultural heritage. This heritage is transmitted directly by parents and indirectly
through friends, acquaintances, symbols, and authority
figures in the community. The total social and cultural environment accounts for the ground rules of
conduct which an individual absorbs to curb and
civilize his or her natural impulses.

Marking the limits of a given culture, it has
been noted, is done by examining the extent to which
individuals internalize a socially unifying idea.
When individuals fail to accept the basic ideas out
of which a culture develops, the limits of that culture have been established. Conversely, a culture
grows in proportion to the quality of the ideas which
inspire it, and when compatible, life-producing ideas
blend to support a system in which adults can function, a minimal level of quality has been achieved.
Totems, statues, flags, insignia of all sorts give
ideas expression in tangible, capsule form. More
sophisticated symbols, written declarations, manifestos, preserved speeches, and advanced forms of
the media, characterize more complicated and enduring cultures.

Understanding another person's cultural heritage helps in determining how strong or weak that
person is because the more acculturated the individual,
the stronger. For this reason, presumption is always

accorded the person defending the status quo, the cultural or social tradition, and the burden of proof rests on the person wishing to change it. Understanding cultural change in a democratic society requires recognition, however, that a quality idea can be superseded by a better idea, and that tradition can give way to well-supported change. It must be added, if hopes for change on a broad cultural level are to be realistic, truly great thinkers are needed, and the links between them and common citizens must hold. The initial strength of those representing tradition must be offset if change is to occur. But through this process, the minority can become the majority, and young liberals can look forward to becoming older conservatives. Once in this position of strength, it has been observed, they are less and less interested in change.

Based on the above fact, the more removed a person is from tradition, the more liberal and more childlike that person is considered to be, and the reverse is also true: the more politically "in" a person is, the more superior or dominant that person's initial position in communication is thought to be. Persons generally might be categorized in such terms relative to strength and weakness. The conservative might be thought of as the person of greatest strength, the liberal of second greatest strength. The reactionary and radical, since they both advocate great change from the status quo, occupy positions of least strength. In terms of the construct of position drawn in Part I, a continuum from superior through equal to subordinate parallels the continuum from conservative through the moderates in both camps to the liberal position. The ultra-conservative or reactionary and the super-liberal or radical might be compared to "Father Time" and "Buck Rogers" images. Neither is in the mainstream of life, but both must be recognized as existing and having some function from time to time.

So strength and/or weakness can be determined

by ascertaining an individual's general position in a cultural framework as conservative, liberal, reactionary, or radical. Accomplishing this task is aided by recognizing how an individual's views or tendencies relate to time. That is, a person may be ahead, behind, or in step with cultural change; the person's appearance, including dress, the tools or techniques he or she uses, the person's values, and guidelines for behavior all can be dated relative to what is general and current practice. The term reactionary in this context of time refers to a tendency to answer present needs with solutions which have been used effectively in the past but now have been generally discarded. The isolationist in American foreign affairs maintains a reactionary stance, for example, because isolationism, the dominant policy of the United States throughout the nineteenth century, was rejected between World War I and World War II. The term radical, at the other extreme, is applied to solutions which are relatively untried. The person with radical ideas suggests solutions to problems which have no relationship to those traditionally practiced.

The liberal and the conservative both think more in terms of the present than do radicals and reactionaries. The liberal is thought of as offering solutions to problems which are slightly ahead of the times. The suggested ideas or changes in the status quo are related directly to it, the more closely related, the less extreme or more moderate. Tradition, it has been said, is upheld by the conservative. Although minor administrative modifications of the status quo may be suggested, the conservative's ideas do not constitute deep-seated or even important change. To illustrate, events in American political history have shown the Democratic Party to be liberal and the Republican Party to be conservative. The Fair Deal, Square Deal, New Deal, New Frontier, and the Great Society have all been changes in the status quo attempted by Democrats. Republicans, on the other hand, have generally maintained a traditional stance toward issues of national importance. In regard to civil rights, government subsidies, and federal controls, Republicans have supported the traditional view that normalcy gives the individual the right to decide for himself without government intervention.

These same four classifications are descriptive of the individual's tendencies in the social, economic, religious, and personal realms. If a person's point of view tends to be liberal, he or she tends to be more experimental and less cautious than the conservative. Each person, then, has a general set of mind which might be cast as reactionary, conservative, liberal, or radical, and the degree to which that person is ready to accept change results from an acceptance or rejection of cultural ideals. The communicator, to design ideas effectively, must know what cultural changes are under way and where other people stand in relation to them. Through this awareness, relative positions in terms of strength and weakness are clearly established.

In summary, the individual characteristics of knowledge, interest, emotional stability, belief, and activity as they are modified by social circumstances and cultural heritage serve as guidelines for the communicator who wishes to outline power relationships in communication. Strength is depicted by great knowledge, many and easily concentrated interests, great emotional stability, loyal commitment to beliefs, and consistent and energetic forms of behavior. These characteristics lead to eminence among equals or influence which in turn leads to an investment in the way things are and have been, both in the group or groups with which the individual is aligned and in the culture generally.

Dimension of Cooperation/Competition

Audience analysis involves more than an assessment of power relationships. Indeed, friendliness or hostility may be of considerable, perhaps more immediate, importance.

It was suggested in Part I (p. 7) that, too
often, the differences between the haves and the
have-nots, or the differences between those with
strength and those without, lead to silence-inducing
isolation which results in a greater imbalance of
positions. The greater the imbalance, the greater
the hostility and/or competition between persons.
The converse is true; the closer to equality people
move, the greater the probabilities of cooperation
or at the least productive competition. Searching
for key differences or similarities in knowledge,
interest, emotional stability, belief and activity,
as well as differences or similarities in social
influence and cultural heritage, is an important
process for persons in communication. The results
of such inquiry determine the amount of cooperation/
competition to be expected and figure into the choice
of the most appropriate pattern of communication.

Techniques for Measuring Dimensions

The process of gauging key dimensions (strength/
weakness and cooperation/competition) in persons in
communication has been aided by modern statistical
methods, technological advances, and generally increased concern for audience analysis, most of which
have grown out of studies of communication on the
mass or extrapersonal level. In the autumn months
of presidential election years, for example, poll
questionnaires are carefully administered to measure
public opinion at regular intervals to determine the
effects of the speaking of presidential candidates.
These campaign polls mark only one development in a
long history of audience analysis and adaptation on
the national level. Although they require huge
amounts of time and money, communicators see the need
for response from others in conducting the progress
of persuasive campaigns. They, in turn, respond to
responses.

This development is a relatively recent thing

in the history of communication theory. By comparison, most nineteenth century American theorists gave almost complete attention to the speaker who, in relation to listeners, was far more knowledgable than his modern counterpart. The average nineteenth-century audience knew little about the latest developments in politics and science, and the orator was, as a result, freer to assert himself without informed contradiction. Today's adult listeners, however, are more selective in listening habits and more critical of the ideas heard. Even the least sophisticated has television and the best talent in communication readily available at all times. Accordingly, speakers on any level are more and more pressed to calculate accurately and quickly the relative weights of persons with whom they communicate.

In response to this need, tests aimed at measuring the individual dimensions of strength/weakness have been developed. Attitude scales are employed to compare persons in terms of their beliefs. Achievement tests seek a comparison of individuals on the basis of factual knowledge. In the area of activity, personality tests aim at behavioral characteristics such as aggressiveness, dominance, etc. Aptitude and preference inventories measure interests, general as well as vocational. Most psychologists admit, however, that these instruments should be accompanied by observations made by the trained evaluator since tests in and of themselves only cover a part of the picture and, too often, the least important part.

Observation in interpersonal communications remains the best gauge for the communicator because the audience is present, and in such a situation the administration of a battery of psychological tests is not generally feasible. So, communicators sharpen their critical powers of interpreting, disposing, and evaluating audience reaction through observation before, during, and after communication occurs. The speaker, for example, draws valuable information about others by questioning them before taking the initia-

tive in communication. The speaker may question
acquaintances or friends of the listener ahead of
time or, in a more formal situation, the person who
gave the invitation to speak, thereby using the observations of others. The experienced politician
often talks informally with members of an audience,
preferably opinion leaders, prior to delivering a
campaign address. They provide for the speaker a
preview of what is to come.

Analysis during communication proceeds through
direct observation of important cues an audience gives
consciously or unconsciously to the speaker. A droop-
ing head, the creaking of chairs, sharp glances all
"speak" to the speaker; many designs have been altered
or abandoned to advantage when listeners were closely
observed.

Post communication analysis is important too,
and what listeners do is really more telling than
what they say. When they act in accord with the idea
communicated, what they say is relatively unimportant.
The ultimate test of effectiveness has been met.

Relating Patterns to People

Having delineated types of people and types
of patterns available to the communicator and having
detailed how the various types of both are recognized,
it remains only to indicate which pattern tends to be
the most productive with which person and why.

Notice in Figure 3 the relationships between
people and patterns. Imagine the speaker at the
center of the chart relating to eight distinct types
of people. Notice that directive designs are associated with hostile superiors and friendly subordinates,
and non-directive designs are associated with hostile
subordinates and friendly superiors. Obviously, the
relationships an individual has are not often located
as precisely as the figures in this illustration;

DESIGNS RELATED TO POSITIONS...

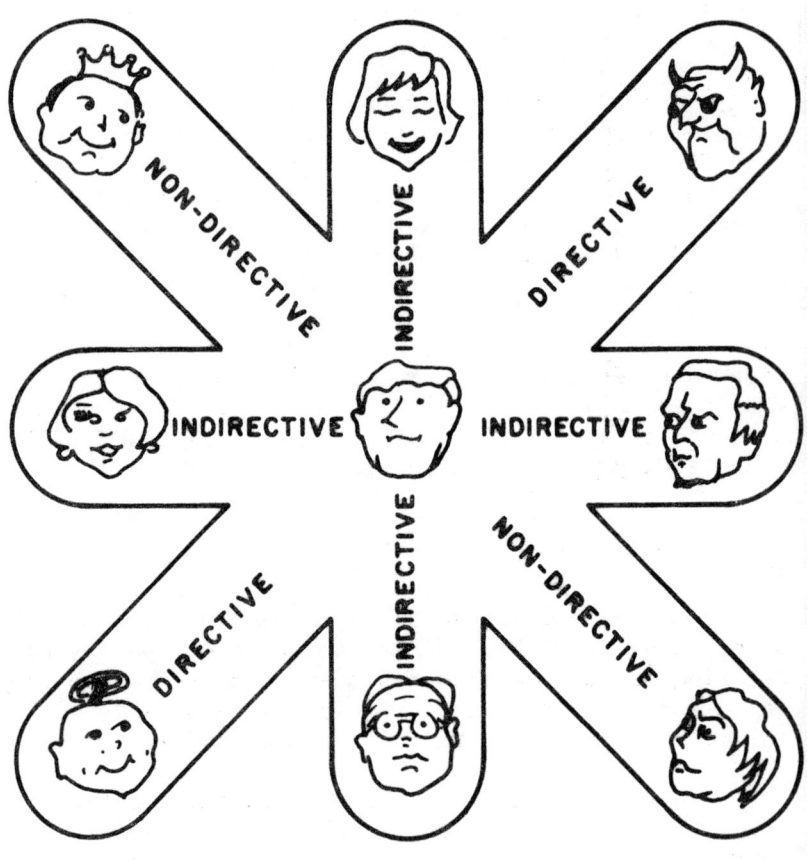

people may fall anywhere on the chart, but some distance in any direction from the center.

In all human relationships when greater equality is achieved, when the subordinate's strength is developed, better ideas result. In a cooperative relationship, the stronger person will employ directive designs; the weaker person will use non-directive designs. In both instances, the advantages of the strengths in a friendly relationship are realized. By making use of the friendly superior's strength, the subordinate gains stature and more closely approaches a position of equality. If, on the other hand, the relationship is hostile, the weaker of the parties involved will find a directive case to advantage in achieving greater equality. If the subordinate were to choose non-direction in this circumstance, it would simply encourage the competitive superior to maintain dominance, regardless of their differences, and the subordinate would never realize his or her own strength/weakness. Not knowing makes equality and better ideas impossible. Also, the emotional damage done by accepting docilely a superior's directive with which one disagrees works against the prospects of continued communication. The stronger person will elicit strength from a hostile subordinate by using non-directive designs. The superior, after all, has nothing to lose and everything to gain. Neutrals and equals will use indirective designs most profitably at the outset of communication.

Persons who are not seeking equality will not communicate to each other for long. If they are forced to communicate, each will rather seek the offices of a third person, usually as a potential partner in communication. It has been noted that two candidates for the same political office will compete, for example, with full knowledge that they both will remain unconvinced by the other's arguments. They speak instead to a third party, and, in actual debate, any attempt to communicate with the other

candidate is recognized as game playing since the
important listener is the voting public. Both
speakers feel that they are strengthening the public by espousing the better idea. The same principle
applies in private kinds of relationships where, for
example, two adults may need others as an audience
before engaging in argument.

    This rationale behind principles guiding the
use of a particular design with a specific listener
or set of listeners is best clarified by reviewing
the impact of traditional relationships in the family
unit upon the communicator. The prototype of the
parent image is characterized as dominant and independent, or superior. The child image is typified
as relatively submissive and dependent, or subordinate. In the cooperative home, the parent directs
and the child questions. As the child matures, the
ratio between his or her age and the age of the
parents diminishes geometrically. In other words,
the father's image at age thirty-five in relation to
his son's, age one, implies great strength, and the
son's image implies a corresponding weakness. When
the son is thirty-five and the father is seventy,
this image-relationship may be reversed. The thirty-
five year old son may be directing the behavior of
the seventy year old father. The father may ask the
son for his advice.

    The development of image relationships, it
should be noted, are more complicated than face value
reveals because, when two people communicate, in
reality at least six immediate images develop. Each
person has an image of himself or herself and an
image of the other person, resulting in a total of
four images; the fifth and sixth images are the
images of the two people as they might be viewed by
an objective observer. Disparities may exist in
these various images over time, but the communicator
relates design to the communicatee on the basis of
his or her best understanding of present images.

As the child grows, other relationships in the family assume meaning. The child relates to uncles, brothers, sisters, and aunts, some strong, some weak, some younger, some older. The image the child holds of the other person in each of these relationships shifts his or her self image. The son, for example, relates to brothers and cousins close to his own age so as to achieve a balanced relationship. He competes or cooperates as an equal, and stronger members of the healthy family encourage such attempts in order to produce a stronger family, individual by individual. Equality and independence are desired.

The creative impulses of childhood, then, are overlaid by the individual's internalization of the critical reflections of family and early societal influences. The adjustments between these creative impulses and critical reflections are made in adolescence, and the active, adaptive adult emerges. This process can be explosive or tranquil depending on the individual adolescent's tendency to emphasize the creative or the critical processes prior to adaptive action in the social context, but the individual who is both creatively active and critically adaptive effects a balance which results in the most productive ideas in an adult society.

When the child communicates his way into the world outside the family structure, he may have already negotiated simultaneous relationships, then, in the role of son, nephew, big brother, little brother, and perhaps even "father." The ability to accomplish this feat, however unconsciously, prepares the individual for relationships with others outside the family which evolve according to the same superior, subordinate, equal images. It has been pointed out earlier (pp. 6-8) that these social relationships are more subtle and less intense than those in the family, and they usually involve more competition. But the fact of position in social relationships is as important as it is in the home, and positions in and principles of communication outside the home parallel those learned in the home. If the child has only been taught abject submission by bone-crunching parents at home, the parents should not be surprised when the child becomes a slave to neighborhood friends and playmates.

Further, images develop and identification occurs outside the home more on the basis of proven merit than on pre-established lines of authority. In open societies, if the communicator has merit, i.e., acts productively upon high quality ideas, others identify themselves with the communicator. Weak adults identify as subordinates; the strong, as superiors. They identify as subordinates, superiors, or equals depending on their own relative strengths and weaknesses.

The child also acquaints himself with the various kinds of designs which accompany power relationships. Directive and non-directive designs are early acquisitions, and, as the individual matures, more and more response is given to designs in the center of the spectrum. Indirect designs require a finer sense of discrimination and greater perspective. The daughter, for example, may realistically need to solve a problem with the indirective help of the mother. They might, then, relate as sisters or equals for a time. It has already been suggested that a parent may spend the last years of life complying with the directives of his or her children.

When the communicator understands these designs and their relationships to images, he communicates as an adult. He or she employs directive design only as the communicatee reveals less information, interest, or ability concerning the idea being discussed. If an equal disagrees, the communicator combs the spectrum toward indirection until the communicatee responds favorably, at which point the communicator realizes the most appropriate design and communicates accordingly. If no agreement is forthcoming, debate ensues.

In the event that a subordinate feels equal
to debate with a superior, he or she should be given
every consideration, every opportunity to show
strength with the hope that subordinate and superior
might work together as equals. Should positions be
reversed, should the subordinate become the superior,
the same principle applies. The subordinate should
be protected in any attempts to change the status
quo.

This explains the suggested use of direction by a competitive subordinate and non-direction
by the superior who recognizes in the subordinate
the urge to compete. Debate may result, or the superior, who admits to the subordinate's stronger
case, may team with the subordinate as an equal and
carry the case to other superiors. A movement may
be underway to change the family, the business, the
community, or the nation with the thought that all
will benefit from the idea.

If an interpersonal relationship is to last,
persons must seek this equality. If they do not, if
the superior uses only direction and the subordinate
only non-direction, then, if nothing else, the in-
firmities of age and the energies of youth will
inevitably surface to disrupt, if not destroy the
relationship. If history has taught human beings
anything, it is the fact that slavery does not work.
The weak must be encouraged to learn, to become
strong, to share the responsibilities of and to direct the course of ideas which effect the community.

Set in this contextual framework, the communicator determines the power of others involved in
communication as well as the competitiveness or
cooperation to be expected and employs the hard,
soft, or no-sale design appropriate to achieving
equality, continuing cooperation, and ultimately
ideas of greater benefit to more people. When in
doubt, the speaker uses indirection, but prepares
all approaches, adapting design on the spot as the

positions of each person involved emerge.

Relating Delivery to Design

When the speaker assumes the position of the advocate, using one of the directive designs with hostile superiors or friendly subordinates, delivery should reinforce the strength of the design. The speaker might stand whenever convention and common sense permit, use relatively strong moves toward an audience, employ gestures which afford emphasis and reveal an aggressive posture. The negotiator, the debater, the advocate must maintain a high energy level. He or she must concentrate interest, fight fatigue, and keep the central idea or specific purpose constantly in the minds of the auditors. The speaker must not apologize or permit weaknesses of the case being developed to occupy the minds of the listeners. All criticisms must be ignored, an extremely difficult task for the persuader who wishes to maintain a self-image of open mindedness and receptivity.

A strong stance is impaired when the persuader suggests that he or she is following directives from superiors, or has difficulties with subordinates, or is facing deadlines anywhere. Indeed, such a stance must not be marred by impatience or bad temper. An attempt should be made, whenever possible, to debate on home ground, geographically and psychologically, and the more friends in attendance, the better. Appearance is also important; the speaker should take care that dress is formal enough for the occasion.

In taking a non-directive position, the reverse usually holds. Unity of design and delivery suggests relatively informal attire, a sitting position even when others may stand, the weaker gestures, the open palm, for example, suggesting submissiveness,

the retreating moves, and a general posture connot-
ing indecision. Interviewing, consulting, providing
information are all situations in which the speaker
purposely attempts to give up strength to elicit
strength from the other person or persons. Scratch-
ing the head, averting the eyes, even closing them,
lowering vocal volume, and using a conversational
tone combine to give the impression of weakness.

       Information, meaning, and a listening atti-
tude should all be stressed when a person assumes a
non-directive stance. The other person's ideas are
given precedence, so the non-directive speaker will
probe, summarize what has been said, and use every
technique to assure the other person that he or she
is getting a fair hearing. Often a note of ambivalence will elicit from the other person a willingness
to take the initiative in the relationship. If what
the other person says runs counter to the persuader's
own beliefs or is based on ignorance, it is either
prelude to directive designs and debate or to non-
directive and indirective designs which will supply
the information or perspective needed by the other
person to operate more on the basis of equality.

       In the indirective designs, equality is
given primacy in delivery. Eye level, dress, movement, gestures, and vocal power reinforce the reciprocity of the situation or a balance of power. Up-
staging or downstaging are inappropriate in this
design. The conference leader, the moderator or
mediator may be the first among equals, but he or
she is among _equals_ and must keep this firmly in
mind so that equality can be clearly translated in
action. Persons sitting around a table to discuss
a common problem reveal by position a need to recognize an equality of status and expected contribution,
equal to equal.

       This last design, indirection, represents
the ideal in communication and should be sought
wherever possible. If time and place, persons and

politics do not permit, then other designs must come into play, but it is the communicator's aim toward equality which provides benefits which are mutual to all in a relationship, ranging from one-to-one interviews to nationally televised speeches.

In summary, the communicator understands that a relationship with others grows if it shows promise of equality and mutual benefit. With this in mind, attempts should be made to employ non-direction with cooperative superiors and competitive subordinates. Direction is most useful with cooperative subordinates and competitive superiors. Initially, indirection is most appropriate with neutrals and equals.

While it is true that some people in a relationship wish to dominate for better or worse and some wish to submit for no good reason, these attitudes lead to behavior which is mutually harmful. Using ideas solely to benefit self without regard for the others' well-being and growth does not affirm equality in relationships. Instead, it furthers inequality. The kind of message which results has been properly labelled propaganda. When propaganda is accepted, when ideas are accepted which benefit others at one's own expense, the individual prostitutes himself. He or she enters into a transaction where much is given for little or nothing in return.

All should benefit from communication. The advocate should believe in his or her own position of strength as it will, indeed, serve others. The interviewer should honestly anticipate greater strength as a result of answers to questions put to others. Participants in conference should be ready to give and take as equals to produce an idea of quality that benefits and is accepted by all.

CONCLUSION

It was suggested earlier that there are qualifications which should be taken into account in using the model of communication offered here. The first qualification relates to the honesty and normalcy of the persons communicating. Using direction with cooperative subordinates and competitive superiors assumes that both dimensions, strength/weakness and cooperation/competition, are honestly represented by both the communicatee and the communicator. When the daughter, for example, gives the impression she is truly understanding and/or accepting what is being said and does not, the mother's sincerely given directions will not engender equality in the relationship. The daughter does not profit through increased strength, and, if the mother expects compliance with the directions given, the realities of the situation will usually prove her wrong, thereby weakening her position as well as the daughter's.

Under certain prescribed circumstances, of course, persons communicating are expected to assume socially prescribed roles, and the normal person will accept a reasonable amount of ceremony as necessary to the successful functioning of an organized society. Teaching, for example, or any other professional role requires that persons involved in communication assume weaker or stronger positions than is true to the facts in order to help others experiment with what may be for them unusual positions in a relationship, and since the professional who assumes a role is not primarily concerned with power relationships, fear of unusual loss becomes irrelevant.

The same is true of the student or any person who is being given help. In a situation of this sort, abnormality would consist of disregarding social roles. If a teacher, for example, cannot acknowledge or accept a student's desire, ill-founded or not, to teach the teacher, and the teacher continues to play the role of the superior, the situation is apt to degenerate into a hopeless confusion which may never be sorted out to anyone's satisfaction. This explains the student's apprently superior position when he or she answers the teacher's question, superior to subordinate. The teacher has assumed the weaker position, and the student has played the stronger role in this transaction. In this case, the "dishonest" question is accepted by both student and teacher as part of an unusual situation.

Abnormalities enter into communication in many ways. If a personality difference is so out of the ordinary as to preclude normal forms of symbolization, then fight or flight, love or hate, and other imponderables result, making any attempt to apply the model of communication developed here unrealistic. The ethical considerations in communication grow out of a recognition of this qualification, and the adult in society must give special study to whether or not parents and children, superiors and subordinates are honestly not only what they seem to be but whether or not they are normal members of society. If they are not normal, the principles of persuasive design suggested here do not apply.

Another qualification involves the extremely large audience which requires extrapersonal techniques, i.e., the mass audience. When a speaker is addressing a nation on television, it is virtually impossible to gauge with precision the key dimensions of the audience. All sorts of friends and enemies, strong and weak, separate and together exist in the audience on such an occasion. In light of this fact, the application of the model on the mass level needs great qualification. It is for this reason that the model has been referred to as an interpersonal model with only suggestive relationships to communication on the extrapersonal level.

The final major qualification is required when the relative values of persons in communication are considered. An individual may honestly and with a sense of normalcy reject equality as a value. Dictatorships offer such a person an arena for action, and, while position is tremendously important in such a society, the individual's object, it seems, is the use of position for mutual harm, not benefit. Directive designs are associated only with superiors, and non-directive designs are used only by subordinates. Little regard is given to the subordinate with a better idea, except to assure the superior that the subordinate does not reap its benefit. Followers are locked into a position of weakness by a leader who, whether stronger or not, retains a dominant role in the relationship. The criterion for judging what is powerful and therefore of value is a predetermined position or rank on the power hierarchy. In this case, the follower's only recourse is to bring down the leader which many dictators have attempted to prevent by assuming divine rights, the last word in a relationship geared to mutual harm.

The person, then, who wishes to persuade must recognize these qualifications. With great patience and a faith in probabilities, the persuader must face the conflict or crisis situation as well as those which are more pleasant as a person dedicated to equality in communication relationships. Each move in practice is judged in this light. Are positions as balanced as possible? If so, better ideas will result, and, if not, the imbalance must be rectified to achieve better ideas for the benefit, or improvement, of all.